HSC ENGLISH

POETRY
COMMON TEXTS

JUDITH BEVERIDGE

SAMUEL TAYLOR COLERIDGE

ROBERT FROST

ROBERT GRAY

Wendy Michaels

PASCAL
PRESS

Wendy Michaels is an educational consultant. Former teacher, English inspector at the Board of Studies and National Education Director of the Shakespeare Globe Centre, she currently lectures at Macquarie University and writes educational material and fiction for young children.

Copyright ©1999 Wendy Michaels

ISBN 186441376X

Pascal Press
PO Box 250
Glebe NSW 2037
(02) 9557 4844

http://www.pascalpress.com.au

Typeset by Artwork Express

Printed in Australia by McPherson's Printing Group

Contents

Contents

Introduction

Students taking the HSC examination in either 2 Unit General English or 2 Unit Related English must study two texts from at least one part of Section I of the Responses to Literature section of the course. These sections are: Poetry, Novel and Drama.

This study guide provides assistance for those students who are studying two texts in Part A: Poetry. There are four poets listed for study in this section of the course in 1999. They are:

> Judith Beveridge
> Samuel Taylor Coleridge
> Robert Frost
> Robert Gray

In this section of the course you are required to study two poets. For each poet a number of poems is listed for study. You are required to study each of the poems set for study for the two poets selected. The poets have been selected in part because they have some aspects in common. They also differ in many ways. While you are not necessarily required to make a series of comparisons between the two poets, it is important to study their poems, noting any areas of similarity and differences.

This study guide is organised in six sections, as follows:

Section

1

Studying Poetry

When you study poetry it is a somewhat different experience from studying other literary forms such as the novel, short story or drama. Poems are a genre of literature in which the poet manipulates a particular form of language (for example, narrative, reflective, lyric) to convey a particular point of view on a subject. Poems tend to be more personal than other literary forms and may even be quite autobiographical. However, you are not required to use the study of a poem as a means of determining the poet's biography, but rather to explore the ideas and feelings of the poem and the ways in which these are expressed.

Just as plays tend to show rather than tell stories, poems also show the poet's ideas and feelings about the subject of the poem. Moreover, they may show it in a variety of forms. The choice of form into which a poet shapes his or her ideas and emotions depends on a number of factors including the personal situation of the poet as well as the historical position in which he or she is situated. While you do not necessarily need to study the historical, cultural and literary period in which the poet is writing you may find it useful to know something of this background, particularly if you are studying a poet such as Coleridge or Frost. The ideas and issues of the poem can, and indeed, must be translated and interpreted by each reader in terms of the time in which the reader is living.

Poetry is a very old literary form. It has been used as a public means of communicating ideas, feelings and events, as well as a private means of expressing an individual's inner being.

Poetry works by concentrating language so that multiple resonant meanings are compacted within the form. The analysis of poetry requires the unpacking of the ways in which the ideas and emotions are concentrated into the form.

Originally poetry was primarily an oral art and it depended on the orator to deliver the lines to a listening audience. Today public presentation of poetry still exists in song lyrics and in some public presentations and readings of poetry. The four poets set for study in this elective illustrate the capacity of poetry to deal with public issues as well as private feelings compacted into lively forms. All the poems listed for study gain from being read aloud. Reading aloud particularly helps the listener to hear and feel the mood and tone and to determine the ways in which the sounds and rhythms contribute to this. Each poem focuses on issues of concern in the period in which the poet is writing and reveals personal views about the issues.

The poem on the page

In studying poems on the page it is important to experience the poem sensually — to hear the sounds of the poem, to visualise the images of the poem and to feel the rhythms of its movement. This is best achieved by reading the poem aloud, or listening to it read aloud, by someone who has been trained in voice and speech. Because the poem's meaning is contained within the form of the poem, it is important to experience that form as the words are shaped in sounds and rhythms. It is sometimes useful to explore the shape and structure of the poem in order to understand the meanings in the poem. In the final analysis it is important to ask:

What is the poem saying?
How does it say this?

The section on each poet in this study guide aims to help you determine this for each poem that you study. Each section contains some introductory contextual information on the poet. For each poem there is a description of the poem that provides you with an outline of what the poem is saying. This is followed by a section of analysis that discusses how the poem communicates its message and mood.

Studying the poems using this study guide

The poets dealt with in this study guide have some aspects in common but they also differ in many ways. In studying the two poets for the examination it is important that you study each poem of each poet individually. You may then look at the similarities and differences amongst the poems written by each poet. A final stage may involve an examination of any general similarities or differences between the two poets that you are studying. This process will assist you to see the critical aspects of each poem and each poet, to clarify the issues raised and to explore the ways in which these issues are presented by each poet.

After you have studied all the poems by the two poets, you should work through section 6 of the study guide that shows you how to look at the two poets side by side and how to write essays that deal with the two poets.

In the final analysis, your study of the poets should enable you to clearly articulate your interpretations of each of the poems by each of the poets, both individually and in relation to one another. To do so you should be able to answer these questions about each poem:

> **what** issues and ideas is each poem communicating?
> **what** feelings or emotions about these ideas are expressed?

how are these communicated through the poetic structures and features?

You should also be able to make some generalisations about the poems of each poet from your study of the set poems. This will enable you to draw conclusions about the general issues and ideas that concern the poet, the various feelings that he or she has about these general issues and ideas and the poetic structures, features, techniques and devices that each poet commonly employs to express and communicate these ideas and feelings. Once you have done this you should be able to answer any question asked in the examination.

Judith Beveridge

Introduction

Judith Beveridge is a contemporary Australian poet. Born in London in 1956, she has lived in Australia since the age of three. Her father came from a fishing village in northern Scotland and her mother came from a village near Birmingham. The family migrated to Australia under the 'assisted passage' scheme and she attended school in Sydney and graduated with a Bachelor of Arts in Communications.

As a school student she disliked traditional poetry and it was only when she came across the confessional poems of Robert Lowell that she began to write poems imitating that form and style. She describes her early confessional poems as self-centred diary entries that concentrated on the problems of her love life. From this beginning she went on to read very widely and to explore the work of many contemporary poets such as Sylvia Plath and Peter Skrzynecki. She kept on writing poetry, experimenting to find her own voice in her first anthology, *The Domesticity of Giraffes*. She has published widely in magazines and anthologies.

Judith Beveridge is married to Surinder Joson; their son, Phillip, was born in 1989. This event caused a minor interruption to her writing of poetry, but she has returned to it and is preparing a second volume of poems that deal less with the natural world and are more concerned with human subjects. She also teaches writing and engages in other part-time positions while writing poetry.

Beveridge is acknowledged for her reflective meditations. She focuses on an object or incident and uses the description of this incident to explore wider meanings. She provides vivid, illuminating descriptions of the particular object or incident, sometimes homing in on an unexpected aspect with a degree of frankness that is surprising. The ideas and issues which she explores reverberate beyond the particular to the wider world and they take on a deeper existential meaning. But this does not mean that her poems lack humour. Beveridge writes with a wry humour that often has a quick sting in its tail.

The Domesticity of Giraffes

This poem gives its title to the collection of poems by Judith Beveridge. This book of poems has been highly acclaimed in literary circles. It won the Dame Mary Gilmore Award and both the NSW and Victorian Premier's Awards for Poetry in 1988. This poem paints a picture of giraffes in their enclosure in the Taronga Park Zoo in Sydney. It is a picture that is filled with pathos as she meditates on their 'domesticity'.

Description

The following outline of the subject of the poem shows you how the poet's ideas are structured. You should use it to help you in your first reading of the poem and then explore and analyse how the poet expresses these ideas and feelings.

	Stanza 1
lines 1–4	introduce the female giraffe and describe her eating with her tongue slowly swinging from side to side as she chews and licks salt from the top of the wire cage in Taronga Park Zoo

| lines 5–8 | describe her imprisonment in this enclosure as confusing to her as she looks over to the tall sheds; she thinks that they are part of a herd because they have paintings of giraffes on them |

Stanza 2

| lines 1–4 | show the poet thinking about the giraffe in her natural environment and imagining her movements in the freedom of that situation |
| lines 5–7 | describe the skin of the giraffe and show the poet speculating that she would look like a bird about to take to the air as she runs in her natural habitat |

Stanza 3

| lines 1–3 | contrast the last image with the present situation in which the giraffe is effectively crippled and unable to run |
| lines 4–7 | describe her repetitive actions in the pen, licking the wire and mimicking the 'gum-chewing audience', standing there in the 'stained underwear of her hide' |

Stanza 4

| lines 1–5 | extend the image of the tongue being like a 'dying bird', with the poet offering her fresh salt from her hand and the giraffe's tongue rolling over the hand in the way that it does over the wire 'in sensual agony' |
| lines 6–9 | describe the male giraffe urinating on the concrete |

▨▨▨▨▨▨▨▨▨ Stanza 5

lines 1–2 | describe how the female giraffe puts her tongue out to take some of the moisture from the male's urine to wet her tongue so that she can go on chewing

Analysis

This poem gives its title to the published collection of poems by Judith Beveridge. It signals some of the key issues that concern her — domestic situations and animals in the natural world. In this case the animals are giraffes whose domestic situation should be the open plains of Africa. But these giraffes have their home in the enclosures of Sydney's Taronga Park Zoo. They are domesticated in the sense of being tamed and the poem questions the effects of this 'domesticity' on the animals.

The poem is structured in five uneven stanzas. The first stanza establishes the situation in which the giraffe finds herself. The second stanza contrasts this situation with an imagined image of 'her plain'. The third and fourth stanzas bring the reader back to the giraffe in the zoo. The enjambed line at the end of the third stanza accentuates the sense of the never-ending incarceration of the giraffe.

The key images of the poem are those associated with the physical appearance of the animals. There is a contrast between the image of the animal that the poet sees and the image that she imagines would be the case were the animal in its normal domestic habitat. The opening image is of the female giraffe's tongue, which is swinging back and forth and is likened, in the simile, to 'a black leather strap'. The images of the tongue licking the salt from the wire and the rolling 'neck of a dying bird' reach a climax with the tongue rolling over the hand which the poet holds out to her. Her eyes are depicted as wounded in the metaphor 'bruised-apple' and their incapacity for seeing accurately is established through the image of her hazy 'gaze' and her inability to detect the unreality of the painted images of giraffes on the wall of the shed. The image of her legs as 'telegraph poles' and the image of her coat as 'stained underwear' further accentuates her stark and desperate situation. The final image of the giraffe bending down to drink the urine being expelled from the 'bull' evokes a sense of pathos for her desperate situation.

This picture of the animal trapped within the zoo along with the life which she might have been leading on the plains is captured in the contrasting vibrant images. The poet describes the movement of her legs in terms of the distance that she might be travelling — 'one long-legged mile after another'. Her head is presented majestically as 'framed in a leafy bonnet'. This domestic image of the human bonnet is at odds with the human-determined existence that she is leading in the zoo. Her hide is also contrasted in an image that draws upon a human domestic situation — 'a paved garden'. This accentuates the alienating effect of the zoo environment. The contrast is given a further poignancy with the comparison of the giraffe in the wild to a 'big slim bird just before flight'. The sense of beauty and freedom associated with these images of her imagined existence is starkly contrasted with the reality of her existence in the zoo.

The contrasts are also established with the images of movement in the poem. These are reflected particularly in the verbs associated with the giraffe. In the enclosure the giraffe 'languorously' '*swings*' her tongue, 'endlessly *licks*', '*ruminates*', '*circles* the pen', '*mimics*', '*rolls* out her tongue', and '*thrusts* her tongue'. These movements suggest a sameness, a monotony, and a crippled kind of movement, echoed in the image of her as 'a wire-cripple'. In the description of her plains life the images suggest, rather than establish, her movement. Thus the image of 'one long-legged mile after another' suggests her freedom of movement and the capacity to cover long distances. The image of her head 'balloon-bobbing in trees' also suggests a lightness and freedom of movement as she grazes amongst the trees. The final image of her 'running' like 'a big slim bird just before flight' accentuates these images of liberty and gracefulness.

There is a further contrast with the bull giraffe. He is mentioned only in the last three lines of the penultimate stanza. His only action is to urinate. The adverb used to describe this action is 'indolently', suggesting a sluggish indisposititie to undertake any activity at all. The image of the 'pink gladiolus' is starkly contrasted with the pallid image of the concrete that is drenched by the stream of urine from the penis.

The images of chewing and licking permeate the poem. Chewing and licking are usually associated with the notion of maintaining life. There is an irony in the fact that the giraffe's licking is for the salt that is blown in from the harbour spray, and the chewing is mimicking the 'gum-chewing audience'. Most significantly, the final thrusting out of the tongue is 'to get moisture for her thousandth chew'. The pathos of this image is accentuated by the word 'thrust', which normally has sexual connotations but which is here associated with utter impotence.

As she explores the situation of the giraffes, domesticated in the Taronga Park Zoo, and compares this with their natural domestic situation, Beveridge faces the reader with a moral question about the ethics of caging animals. The distorted actions of the female giraffe in particular become the focus of the poet's questioning. The reader is left wondering whether there is any justification for this kind of domesticity.

Using the description and analysis in this study guide **and** your own reading of the poem make your own set of notes that answer these questions:

- **what** issues and ideas is the poem communicating?
- **what** feelings or emotions about these ideas are expressed?
- **how** are these expressed in the poetic form, features, techniques and devices?

Orb Spider

'Orb Spider' is a gentle meditation in which the poet uses her observations of the spider spinning her web in the afternoon light to reflect on aspects of her own life and the wider universe. It is a poem in which the poet almost becomes the subject as she watches and learns from the spider. The poem supports the notion that all things in the natural world are sacred and should be treated with due respect.

Description

The following outline of the subject of the poem shows you how the poet's ideas are structured. You should use it to help you in your first reading of the poem and then explore and analyse how the poet expresses these ideas and feelings.

| lines 1–2 | describe the orb spider spinning a web in the pale light |
| lines 3–4 | describe the sounds of the insects in the bushes |

lines 4–5	comment that some of these insects will soon be eaten by the spider
lines 6–8	describe the beauty of the spider as she spins the web
lines 8–11	describe how the web is designed to catch a bee and thread it back onto the flowers
lines 12–14	describe the spider suspended in the shadows of the setting sun
lines 14–15	describe the petals of the flowers moving in unison
lines 16–20	describe how the poet watches the spider creating her own world and her own world view
lines 20–23	comment on the effect that this has on the poet's view of her world
lines 24–28	comment on how this experience of watching the spider has made the poet view the skies and their patterns quite differently
lines 19–32	comment that the spider taught the poet to love the smallest aspects of the universe
lines 33–34	describe the spider making her perfectly shaped web

Analysis

This poem is a delicate meditation on the universe of the spider which is used by the poet to explore her understanding of the broader universe in which she moves. This poem is spun out like the spider's web, thread by thread, as she pieces together the meanings of her observations.

The poem is structured in three parts. The first part is concerned with the poet's observations of the spider 'pegging our her web' and the connections that she makes with the plants around her world. In this section the poet speculates on the future fate of insects which will be caught in her web. The second section is concerned with the poet's observations of the spider as she completes the task of constructing her web. This leads the poet to meditate upon the significance of these observations for her own life. The third section projects these meditations onto a larger canvas as the poet connects the spider, her life and the wider universe in the notion of 'one perfect drawing'.

The word 'orb' denotes the shape of a sphere or globe. Both these words also imply the world. The orb-weaving spider is one of the spiders of the genus Araneus which weave an orb-shaped web each night. The weaving of this web usually takes place at dusk as the light is fading. The purpose of the web is to catch night-flying insects for food. The poet is playing on all these meanings in the poem as she places the cosmological image of the web at the centre of the poem. Beveridge uses the image of cosmography to expand the idea of the spider to encompass her own world. Cosmography, literally, denotes the science which describes and maps the heavens and earth and represents the wider universe. And this is what Beveridge is doing in the poem, as she meditates on the significance of doing it. The image is given further significance as the metaphor is extended to take in the notion of 'planetismal' which denotes the minute bodies that move in orbits and gradually unify to form a solar system. These key ideas reverberate through the other images which Beveridge connects to them.

The spider produces her own 'known world' and this world is 'a little portion of the sky'. The image of the web that is 'drawn/ by the smallest nib' suggests that the orb spider is constructing a map of the world that she inhabits. The world that the spider constructs, like the pattern of the heavens, has a 'pattern like a matchbox puzzle'. This image of the puzzle suggests an intricate complexity in the world of the spider, and in the planetary world. The pattern is likened to the 'tiny balls' in the 'matchbox puzzle' which are loose and move apparently without purpose and direction — until they suddenly, almost inexplicably, find their 'place'. The poet uses this image to explore the key idea in the poem of her own understanding of 'the smallest transit'.

The poet herself is, in one sense, the subject of the poem. There is a strong pattern of verbs in the poem that shows the mental activity of the poet. These verbs are all connected with the mental act of seeing and understanding — '*saw*', '*watched*', '*could see*' and '*knew*'. Towards the end of the poem, the poet locates the source of her gathering insight in the active teaching of the spider. The poet says that the spider 'taught' her 'to love the smallest transit'. Watching the spider she learned the significance of this small movement within the world. She writes of learning 'that the coldest star has a planetismal beauty'. The poet's understanding is expanded beyond the watching of the spider to a comprehension of her own world. The spider's web has become for the poet 'one perfect drawing'.

The spider has a duality to her life. She is involved in both movement and stillness as she spins and pegs out her web and 'trusses up insects'. The spider is also able to 'dance in the sky'. There is a suggestion here of the cruelty of the spider that is admired by the poet. Set against this is a capacity for stillness as the spider hangs 'in the shadows'. In all this the spider is revered for her capacity to 'produce her known world' as she creates her web.

The web is captured in images such as 'thin as a pressed flower in the bleaching light'. It is at once beautiful and lethal. The poet writes of the way in which the web could catch an insect and gather it up, threading it onto the adjacent flowers. This image of the power of the web and its beauty is juxtaposed with other images such as the 'tiny balls stuck in a grid'.

The other key players in this drama are the insects and plants and the sky. The insects are 'small'; noisy — 'clicked like opening seed-pods'; and vulnerable — 'would be trussed up' and 'threaded onto the flower/ like a jewel'. The plants provide a splash of colour in the poem. The 'bright marigolds' appear 'more apricot' and 'more amber', and the small petals 'moved as one flame'. This warmth and colour is contrasted with the images of coldness in the 'bleaching light' of the sky and the 'coldest star'. The sky is the backdrop against which the drama of the spider spinning her web is carried out. The sky also becomes the subject of the poem as the poet extends the metaphor of the poet's web to the 'dance in the sky'.

As she engages in this meditation the poet draws the reader into the world of the spider. This world becomes a metaphor for the known world of the poet and the poet seems to be placed at the centre of this meditation. The reader comes to understand, through the poet's own process of gaining understanding, the significance of the tiniest phenomena in the scope of the universe.

Activity

Using the description and analysis in this study guide **and** your own reading of the poem make your own set of notes that answer these questions:

- **what** issues and ideas is the poem communicating?
- **what** feelings or emotions about these ideas are expressed?
- **how** are these expressed in the poetic form, features, techniques and devices?

Streets of Chippendale

Chippendale is an inner-city area of Sydney. In its earlier days it was a precinct of the well-to-do, but it has since deteriorated as a locality, with the building of factories and hotels dominating the area. Chippendale, at the time that the poet was writing, was seen as a somewhat dangerous place in which to walk the streets and a place inhabited by undesirables, derelicts and criminals.

Description

The following outline of the subject of the poem shows you how the poet's ideas are structured. You should use it to help you in your first reading of the poem and then explore and analyse how the poet expresses these ideas and feelings.

Lines 1–5	identify the names of streets in Chippendale communicate the impression of homeliness that these names evoke comment that these streets are now treeless and changed by the presence of factories
lines 6–9	comment on the impression given by the name Abercrombie
lines 10–14	comment that the reality of Abercrombie is very different from the impression that the name gives
lines 15–19	contrast the expectations about the people who might be in this street and those who do actually use it
lines 20–21	comment on the ruin that has hit Abercrombie street

lines 22–26	contrast the expectations about Abercrombie Street and its reality
lines 26	comment on the change of character that streets do undergo
lines 27	comment that this change also happens to suburbs
lines 28–29	comment that none of the present inhabitants of these streets mourn these changes
line 29	comment that Christian names have no meaning
lines 30–33	comment that surnames of people are featured in police files

Analysis

The poem is structured in eight quatrains. Within some of the stanzas there is a suggestion of half rhyme — 'crosses/terraces' — in the first and third lines, giving a sense of an attempt to keep the place in order. However the lack of rhyme in the other lines and in some stanzas seems to overwhelm the poem and suggest the inevitability of change. The use of enjambed lines that run across the stanzas helps to reinforce this idea. There is a subtle interplay between past and present in this poem which further highlights the notion of change.

Beveridge uses the extended metaphor of the names and personalities of the streets to explore the notion of change. Each street is personified and given the particular qualities of the name. These are grouped to identify their distinctive qualities. The first group of names include 'Ivy, Vine, Rose and Myrtle'. These streets, with their feminine names, are associated with the natural world. However, the streets that bear these names 'now lack a single tree'. There is a sense of loss associated with this that is highlighted in the grammatical metaphor — 'lack' (the metaphor is contained in the verb). The association of these names with 'kindly aunts in quiet suburbs' gives them an aura of otherworldliness and gentility which serves to underpin the nature of the loss that has come with change.

The other feminine name, 'Caroline', is presented as something of a 'dark lady' as she is described as 'Sad daughter of the ruined slipper'. She is also connected with the 'pub-crawlers that back on' to her and with 'a mass of work-boot bruises'.

Contrasted with these names are those associated with male identities. These include 'Hugo, Louis', 'Thomas and Edward'. 'Thomas and Edward' have 'climbed' the social ranks 'to renovated villas'. 'Hugo' and 'Louis' should be 'respected gentlemen', but they are actually 'beer mates' of Abercrombie and 'pub crawlers' who associate with the less-than-reputable Caroline.

The main street in Chippendale is Abercrombie Street. The poet comments on the use of a surname for this street, a name that resembles an 'eccentric, unmarried third cousin'. The name suggests the casual refinement of 'residents dressed in slacks and turtlenecks' and 'pedigree dogs'. Abercrombie Street does not, however, live up to these expectations. It 'hits the bottle', 'grumbles', 'screeches' and 'lands in trouble with the police'.

Beveridge uses these different characterisations of streets as a meditation on change. The streets that once housed the suburb's gentry, as evidenced in the names and their associations, are now changed almost beyond recognition. The 'loss' is so permanent that there is no one to even 'mourn' it. This thought is further expanded as the poet comments that 'Christian names mean nothing'. The individuals who once gave their names to the streets are not remembered.

However, surnames do not disappear as easily as Christian names. Beveridge contrasts Abercrombie Street with the other streets named after individuals suggesting that the family name is the one that is recorded — particularly in the 'police files'.

In this meditation, the poet stands outside and observes and comments. She looks back to the past and contrasts that with the present. She describes the suburb of Chippendale that has gone 'to the wall' following the moving in of the 'factories like terrible relations'. In one sense this is a meditation on the ways in which progress does not necessarily bring prosperity or gentility. Change, in this suburb, has been damaging — not only to the character of the place but also to people who might 'stray into one of its dark corners'.

 ctivity

Using the description and analysis in this study guide and your own reading of the poem make your own set of notes that answer these questions:

- **what** issues and ideas is the poem communicating?
- **what** feelings or emotions about these ideas are expressed?
- **how** are these expressed in the poetic form, features, techniques and devices?

The Two Brothers

This poem is a meditation on masculine sexuality. It is a personal account told from the point of view of a young girl who is looking back on an earlier time of her life in which she was tormented by these two brothers. It is important to remember that this young girl may not necessarily be the poet and that the poem should not necessarily be seen as autobiographical. In the process of the meditation we see the gender differences that emanate from the different physical make-up of male and female. Despite the criticisms of the boys, the poet also expresses some sympathy for their situation.

Description

The following outline of the subject of the poem shows you how the poet's ideas are structured. You should use it to help you in your first reading of the poem and then explore and analyse how the poet expresses these ideas and feelings.

Stanza 1

describes the two brothers and their cruelty to animals

Stanza 2

describes the ways that the brothers used to torment the girl and how she collected snails and hid them from the brothers

Stanza 3

comments on how the snails provided the girl with endless moments of fascination

Stanza 4

describes the girl's reaction to the boys' cruelty to the snails

Stanza 5

describes the torture that the brothers inflicted on the snails as the girl watched in horror

Stanza 6

> continues the description of the torture of the
> snails and comments on the dead birds that
> the boys carried in their pockets

Stanza 7

> comments on the brothers' lack of feeling
> and identity underlying their cruelty to animals

Analysis

In this poem the poet takes on the persona of a young child whom we assume to be a girl. She paints a vivid picture of the girl in her interactions with the two boys (who are brothers). We come to understand the power relations between the two sexes that are reflected in the behaviour of these young children and the collusion between the two boys. The poem is structured in seven unrhymed quatrains. Beveridge makes use of enjambement both within stanzas and across stanzas and this increases the sense of the power of the boys in their interactions with the young girl.

The girl and her observations of the boys are the main focus of this poem. The girl 'collected snails' and her observations of their behaviour show her capacity for compassion and empathy. She 'hid' the snails in the 'neglected part of the garden' to keep them away from the boys. Her perception of the snails was focused on their fairytale-like existence. She was fascinated by their very existence and describes how 'a single leaf' was sufficient to 'paint picture-books' for her. The magical qualities of the snails are revealed in the image of the 'two wands at their heads touching'. The image of the snails 'delicately' drawing back into their shells also reveals the fascination which these tiny creatures had for the child. Her handling of the snails is sharply contrasted with the boys' attitudes to the tiny creatures of the natural world.

The images associated with the boys are of cruelty and torment. The boys kill lizards, cause sparrows to bleed by pricking them with 'a needle', and cause excruciating pain to the snails by sprinkling them with salt and pushing twigs into them. There is an arrogance in the way that the boys would 'dare each other any taste, any soft clot, any ugly act'. This crucial image captures the notion of masculinity within the poem. It is a brazenly uncaring attitude towards other living things. Coupled with this cruel attitude to living creatures is a sense of threat to the girl, a threat to impose themselves on her if she exposes their actions by crying out loud or by telling on them.

The most potent images in the poem are those of the boys' sexuality. The poet describes how the boys had 'shown me themselves', and how this showing had been accompanied by their 'grinning queerly'. This image is amplified as the poet desribes how 'they touched themselves' and 'held themselves in their hands' and how this left them with a feeling of bewilderment and fear. The bewilderment is associated with the boys' lack of understanding of the power of their possession and the fear that this possession might be less than it seemed.

Despite the sense of terror that the girl experiences, there is a depth of understanding on her part that surpasses the boys' perceptions of their situation. Her criticisms are both harsh and gentle. She recounts the cruelty of the boys' actions in a straightforward manner. She is simply 'telling it as it is'. The boys, 'big with the world/in their pockets', have an apparent strength and capacity to inflict injury and torment on their victims; yet they do not understand the force that is driving them and the underlying fear that 'they'd find the prize of nothing'. The simplicity of the recount magnifies the horror of the boys' actions.

In this meditation on masculine sexuality the poet evokes a

sense of sympathy for the boys' dilemma. While their actions are horrible, and their collusion in these actions seemingly inexcusable, the poet allows the reader to see something of their dilemma as they lack a real understanding of power and its appropriate uses. Beveridge locates this lack of understanding in the boy's sexuality and shows how this enables them to carry out the kinds of actions that she describes in the poem. Like the poet, we do not condone these actions, but we comprehend the boys' situation.

Using the description and analysis in this study guide **and** your own reading of the poem make your own set of notes that answer these questions:

- **what** issues and ideas is the poem communicating?
- **what** feelings or emotions about these ideas are expressed?
- **how** are these expressed in the poetic form, features, techniques and devices?

Fox in a Tree Stump

'Fox in a Tree Stump' is a personal account of an incident in which the poet experiences extreme fear. She describes the situation in which she is to assist her uncle in killing a fox that has ensconced itself in a tree stump. The poet is merely nine years old at the time of this incident, but there is the sense that the incident itself and her uncle have had an immense influence on her being. In one sense the poem is about the ways in which adults can and do manipulate young children who have no power to resist.

Description

The following outline of the subject of the poem shows you how the poet's ideas are structured. You should use it to help you in your first reading of the poem and then explore and analyse how the poet expresses these ideas and feelings.

Stanza 1

lines 1–3	recount how the girl is standing in a paddock holding a tree branch
lines 4-5	recount how her uncle has driven off leaving her there to beat the fox

Stanza 2

line 6	describes the terror that the girl feels
lines 7–10	comment on the responsibility that the uncle has left the girl with and how he will not understand if she fails in this task

Stanza 3

line 11	describes the girl's fear
lines 12–14	describe how she stood waiting for the fox to appear

Stanza 4

line 15	describes the appearance of the fox
lines 16–21	describe the shot that hit the fox and disturbed the galahs and rabbits in their burrows

Stanza 5

lines 22–23	describe how the uncle disposed of the body of the fox in a ditch

| lines 24–26 | describe the girl's immediate reaction to this incident |
| lines 27–28 | comment on her age and identity |

Stanza 6

| lines 29–30 | comment on the feeling that she has about the incident and her uncle |

Analysis

The poet expresses the feeling of extreme fear in this poem. While the fear is about the fox in the stump, the reader comes to realise that the poet is even more terrified of the uncle himself. There are several images in the poem which communicate this fear. The poem opens with the description of the poet who has 'gripped the branch'. The next image of fear is contained in the metaphor, 'Terror barrel-rode through my stomach'. This gripping image of the panic in her stomach is elicited by her understanding of her uncle and his impatience if she does not succeed in her task. It is this fear which is elaborated upon in the remainder of the poem. The image of 'fox-hairs of dust' that 'sweated' in the palms of her hands and the 'tongue' that reaches 'into a hurting body and strike[s] ashes' continue the sense of terror that the poet is portraying.

The poet establishes the place where the child is waiting in the image of a 'paddock that ran on/over harder and harder earth'. There is a sense of the impenetrability of the ground as well as a feeling of the difficulty of the task ahead. This image is reinforced by additional images such as the 'exhaust of leaves' which suggests a sense of the trees having exhaled the leaves from their branches. In this landscape there is the sound of the 'twig' as it 'snapped' and the noise of the 'flock/of galahs from their trees'.

The harshness of the place is reflected in the harshness of the uncle whom the poet so fears. The uncle's arms are described as 'dry river-beds dammed at the shoulders', his hands are 'quick rabbit-skinning', and his voice is 'harsh, kelpie cursing'. Importantly there is something almost animal-like in the glint that the poet sees in her uncle's eye. This description suggests an almost feral quality to the man. He is harsh, strong, easily angered and dangerous — more dangerous perhaps than the fox.

He moves in and out of the landscape and those movements are described by the poet in the simplest of terms. For instance the first mention of him comes in the clause, 'my uncle drove off'. He later returns and this is simply stated — 'When my uncle came back'. Similarly, there is a simplicity to the way in which she describes the uncle's disposing of the dead fox: 'he threw/the charred body into a ditch.' This is contrasted with the more elaborate images of her fear and the landscape.

In between the description of the harshness of his body and the simple statements of her uncle's actions there is the poet's understanding of how her uncle responds to situations. She 'knew' her uncle well. She knew that he 'would not understand' if she did not get the fox. This statement of her knowledge is particularly interesting. It is the physical features of the uncle that would not understand, rather than the personality or character of the uncle who would not understand her fear.

The dominant image in the poem is the killing of the fox. This is surrounded by the images of the 'smoke' and the 'stick' and the sound that the stick makes as it hits the fox and the sound of the fox coughing. This sound is like a gunshot and the repetition of the word 'shot' emphasises the ringing sound that it makes. The force of the sound is further emphasised in the verbs 'shook' and 'cracked'. These form part of the images that show the effect of the sound on the ground and in the air. The sound of the killing of the fox was so loud that it 'shook out' galahs from a tree and 'cracked like a wave' the sleep of rabbits in their burrows. There is an irony that these two creatures are so disturbed by the death of the fox, as they are prey to this predator.

The prevailing sense of terror in this poem is less concerned with the predatory fox, than with the equally predatory uncle. The young child is affected by the killing of the fox and turns away from the dead body as her uncle throws the remains into the ditch. She expresses her horror as she tries to cover the 'bloodspots of fire' and and prays 'not to waken/another animal from the wheat'. But there is a greater fear in this poem and that is the fear of the uncle who strikes terror into the 'nine years old' child. This is particularly poignantly expressed in the repetition of the image of praying. The first image of praying is concerned with the child praying that she does not disturb any other animals from the wheat fields. The second image is focused on the uncle. The child 'prays for the dark' when she sees 'the sun caught in [her] uncle's eye'. There is a strong sense of the madness that is her uncle, a kind of animal glint that causes her so much distress that she wants only darkness so that it is blotted out.

Beveridge evokes a strong sense of fear in this poem, but the fear is not of the predatory fox, but rather of the young poet's uncle. In one sense this is a meditation on the overwhelming power that adults have over children and the ways in which they can use this power to coerce children. There is also a sense in which the poem demonstrates the lack of insight on the part of the adult into the reaction of the child to the situations in which the adult places her. There is a strong sense of criticism in this poem, but is contained within the simply contrasting images of the fox and the uncle and the overriding fear of the child.

ctivity   Using the description and analysis in this study guide **and** your own reading of the poem make your own set of notes that answer these questions:

- **what** issues and ideas is the poem communicating?
- **what** feelings or emotions about these ideas are expressed?
- **how** are these expressed in the poetic form, features, techniques and devices?

Writing about the poet

After studying each poem individually it is important that you consider the commonalities in the ideas, feelings and poetic features of the poems that you have studied by the one poet. You can do this by considering the following general questions about all the poems and writing notes in answer to the questions using a range of poems to justify your general statements.

- What subjects and ideas does the poet explore in the poetry?
- What emotions or feelings does the poet express in the poetry?
- What forms and structures does the poet commonly use?
- What techniques or devices does the poet commonly use to encapsulate these ideas and feelings?

You should then write an essay such as the following that deals with the poems of this poet in a general way:

- 'Beveridge's poetry provides intensely personal meditations on homely things.' To what extent is this true of the poems that you have studied?

In answering this question you need to:

- define what you mean by 'intensely personal'
- determine the features of 'meditations'
- define what you mean by homely things
- select two poems that allow you to evaluate the truth of the statement
- develop an argument that either supports, negates or qualifies the statement.

Samuel Taylor Coleridge

Introduction

Coleridge was born in England in 1772, the son of a clergyman, and was destined to enter the church as an adult. His father died when he was very young and he was sent away to Christ's Hospital School in London. He refers to this experience in some of his poetry, particularly in 'Frost at Midnight'. As a child he was seen as temperamental and somewhat dreamy but he had an appetite for reading and for talking. He later studied classics at Jesus College, Cambridge. He lived through a turbulent period of history and saw the industrial revolution in England and the French Revolution, enlisting in the 15th Light Dragoons at one point before his brother bought him out under an 'insanity 'clause.

He met and was influenced by some of the great thinkers, poets and philosophers of his time, including William Wordsworth, William Hazlitt, Thomas Carlyle, John Keats and Ralph Waldo Emerson. His friendship with Southey led to the invention of 'Pantisocracy', which intended to set up a utopian commune. He and Southey gave political lectures to raise the finance for this project — but it did not eventuate after he and Southey had disagreements over various financial matters. Coleridge married Sara Fricker and they retired to a cottage at Clevedon where some of his poetry was written and where his first son, Hartley, was born. Hartley is the sleeping child referred to in 'Frost at Midnight'.

Perhaps his strongest friendships and most powerful working relationships were with the Wordsworths — William and Dorothy — whom he met in 1797. Their friendship and professional collaborations were based on their mutual love of walking in nature, reading and writing poetry and philosophising. Some of his most poignant poetry was written during the fourteen years in which these friends collaborated. Indeed it was Wordsworth who suggested that Coleridge write the powerful narrative poem, 'The Rime of the Ancient Mariner', for which he is probably best known as a poet. Together, Wordsworth and Coleridge experimented with English poetry and explored ideas about nature, pantheism and romanticism. Their most significant collaboration was the production of *Lyrical Ballads* in 1798.

By the time of publication of their joint venture, Coleridge had become disenchanted with the course of the French Revolution and went abroad to Germany. At this time his marriage was becoming strained and on his return to England he left his wife and went to live with the Wordsworths in the Lakes district. He had by this stage fallen in love with Sara Hutchison and was hopelessly addicted to opium. Despite attempts to restore his health it deteriorated and this affected his relationships with the Wordsworths and with Sara. He returned to London for a period between 1811 and 1814. It was after this that his Christian beliefs were resurrected and he resumed his writing with surprising energy. He died in 1834 leaving behind an enormous legacy of poetry and other writings.

Romanticism

Romanticism is an important movement in the history of English poetry and philosophy. It took place in the period between 1770 and 1850 as something of a reaction to the 'Enlightenment'. It was inspired by the ideas that fuelled the French Revolution and the American Revolution and other local wars in various parts of Europe. It was also motivated by the beginnings of the industrial revolution and the effects that this was having on human life.

Its key concern was the individuality of human beings and the value of individual, personal and subjective experience. The emphasis on the subjective and on the emotional life necessitated a transformation of English poetry. This included a discarding of tightly controlled poetic structures in order to find forms that would deal with emotionalism and the individual experience. This experience took poets out into the natural world in a way that had not previously occurred. The Romantic Poets were constantly in touch with a world of the senses that gave them access to the world of the spirit. They were concerned with the state of childhood (an innocent state), with the role of memory and the imagination, and with the process of creativity.

But it was not the case that all the poets held identical views about all these aspects of their life and work. Indeed, Wordsworth and Coleridge, despite their close collaboration, held somewhat different views about the presence of the spirit in nature and in human beings. For Wordsworth nature had its own autonomous existence, whereas Coleridge, at least for most of his life, retained the belief that there is one Life or one Spirit for the physical, animal and human worlds.

The notion of the Imagination was a central idea in the work of these poets and they explored it not only through their writing but also debated and wrote about its significance to their work. The Imagination was seen by the poets in general as a means of ordering sense impressions. Coleridge developed the idea of the Imagination and distinguished primary and secondary imagination. According to Coleridge, the primary Imagination makes possible perception and knowledge. The secondary Imagination is the poetic imagination which involves 'deep feeling and profound thought'. It shapes, interprets and recreates experience.

Conversational poems

Coleridge wrote a range of poems including sonnets, ballads, confessional poems and political poems as well as a range of 'visionary framents'. His conversational poems are essential to the Romantic poetry tradition. They embody the kind of autobiographical rumination that was to become identified with the movement. These poems are usually written in blank verse and although called conversation poems they are, in fact, monologues in which the listener is either silent ('The Aeolian Harp'), asleep ('Frost at Midnight') or some distance from the speaking poet ('This Lime-Tree Bower my Prison'). The imagined conversation is with a particular person and the style and form of the poetry was essentially invented for this new poetic purpose.

The poems appear to draw upon the tradition of the eighteenth century verse letter, or 'epistle', and the newly developing form of the Romantic autobiographical meditation. Although the form was invented almost by accident as Coleridge was expressing his frustrations with the existing formalities of the accepted verse forms, he immediately developed the form, first entitling it 'Conversational poem' and later restating it as 'Conversation poem'. He also used the general title 'Meditative poems in blank verse' to describe these poems. The poems are sometimes considered to be a poem sequence, although they are also taken to be individual and distinct in their own right.

In these poems the poet generally commences in the immediacy of the domestic situation and moves out into the landscape beyond. There are moments where this imaginative journey into the landscape allows the poet an insight into the problem or situation that stimulated his initial contemplation. He generally returns to the same domestic situation at the end of the poem, but his views and his mood are changed by the experience. Despite the moments of bleakness in the conversation poems they are essentially optimistic.

Frost at Midnight

This poem is thought to have been written about Coleridge's son, Hartley. The infant is asleep and Coleridge is contemplating the sleeping child. It is midnight and everything else is quiet as the poet sits alone in deep contemplation. This contemplation takes him back to memories of his own childhood and this leads him to ruminating upon the bigger questions of existence.

This poem is written in four stanzas. The movement of the ideas in the stanzas reflects the movement of the conversation with the sleeping child. It begins within the domestic situation of the house at midnight with the absence of all others from the household except for the sleeping infant beside the poet. The movement from this domestic moment goes not only out into the world, but also back into his own childhood before returning to the situation of the silence of the midnight moment and the frost's 'secret ministry'.

Description

The following outline of the subject of the poem shows you how the poet's ideas are structured. You should use it to help you in your first reading of the poem and then explore and analyse how the poet expresses these ideas and feelings.

Stanza 1

lines 1–3 | describe the frost and the owl
| establish the time of night and the silence

lines 4–7 | set the scene, with all the other inmates of the cottage having gone to bed
| establish the poet as awake, musing and contemplating in 'solitude'
| describe his young infant sleeping 'peacefully' at his side

lines 8–10	comment on the extreme calmness of the atmosphere
lines 10–13	describe the surroundings of the village where the cottage is situated comment that they are so quiet that they are 'inaudible'
lines 13–16	describe the only movement in the world as the 'thin blue flame' of the fire that is still burning in the fireplace
lines 17–23	show the poet contemplating the connection between himself and the flame indicate that he seems to be the only human thing not moving in the world and it is the only moving thing in nature describe the flame as a 'companionable form' identify the similarities between the poet and the flame, particularly its flapping movement and his own 'idling Spirit' which plays with his thoughts as though they were a 'toy'

Stanza 2

lines 23–26	indicate that the poet's thoughts are drawn back to his own childhood and his memories of school
lines 26–33	show a new set of thoughts of his past memories coming upon the poet describe some of the experiences of his youth and the memories of his 'birth-place' present the memory of the sounds of the church bells ringing out as music that was predicting 'things to come'

lines 34–35	recall how the poet 'gazed' until he fell asleep and dreamed of these 'soothing things'
lines 36–38	recall how the poet would 'brood' the next day under the stern gaze of the teacher describe how the book which he was supposed to be studying was 'swimming' before his eyes
lines 39–43	describe how the only relief from this school experience was the poet's hope that, when the school-room door opened, there would be the hoped-for appearance of the 'stranger'

Stanza 3

lines 44–47	return to the baby who is lying asleep beside the poet and whose breathing has intruded into the pauses of his thinking describe his feelings of love for the child
lines 48–51	express the poet's joy at his beautiful baby and his feelings of wonderment as he looks at the child indicate his wish that this child shall learn other things from those which he had to learn as a child, and learn them in very different situations
lines 51–53	comment that the poet was brought up in the city where there was very little beauty
lines 54–58	show the poet addressing his sleeping baby, saying that the child will grow up in very different places in the natural world where he will be able to 'wander like a breeze' through Nature

| lines 58–64 | show the poet's belief that the child will be close to God and will be in touch with the 'eternal language' which comes from God |
| | assert that the child will be taught by the 'Great universal Teacher' who will shape his soul, giving it sustenance and enabling it to 'ask' |

Stanza 4

lines 65–70	act as a kind of coda to the poem
	establish the conclusion of the argument that Coleridge has proposed
	assert that because the child will grow up with this experience of nature and learning life will be 'sweet' for him
lines 70–74	return to the silent sounds of nature and the work of the frost where the poem began
	assert that not even the winter will bring harm to this child

Analysis

Coleridge establishes the innocence of childhood through the image of the sleeping infant. He describes the child as his 'cradled infant' who 'slumbers peacefully' and contrasts this with his own childhood experiences which were much harsher because he was not brought up close to the natural world.

The images of the natural world encompass the frost, the landscape, and the creatures of the earth. The frost is first described as having a 'secret ministry'. This word ministry suggests an aiding of the spirit. This ministry is achieved without the assistance of 'any wind' — an image which suggests the power of the frost to induce the atmosphere of calm that pervades the house. The frost image appears again at the end of the poem where Coleridge comments on the power of the frost to create 'silent icicles' which shine 'to the quiet Moon'.

The calm created by the frost, the absence of people and the sleeping infant has another side to it. It is so deeply silent that it 'vexes meditation' and 'makes a toy of Thought'. The thoughts that follow from this quietness and disturbed spirit, however, lead Coleridge eventually back to the belief in the spirit that pervades all of nature and which ensures another kind of peace. He expresses this in the confidence that the seasons will be 'sweet' to his child.

The landscape images include those of the village such as 'sea, hill and wood', which are simply stated and repeated in the first stanza without elaboration. In his recollections of his own childhood there is almost a complete absence of these images as they are replaced by other images. The only reference to the natural world in his memory of his childhood is in the 'sky and stars'. Even his 'sweet birthplace' is remembered by the sounds of the church bells. The images of nature that are to be part of the life of his child are vibrant and flowing with life. The landscape images include 'lakes and sandy shores', 'crags of ancient mountain' and 'clouds' and are augmented with the images of the opposing seasons. Summer is personified as clothing the earth 'with greenness'. In winter the 'redbreast' sings on the bough of the apple tree, providing a strong visual contrast to the white of the snow and ice.

The creatures of the natural world which appear in the poem are connected with the ideas of innocence and joy. They also provide the sounds of the poem. The 'owlet's cry' is the sound that is heard above the great stillness in the beginning of the poem. It is immediately connected with the poet's thoughts about his infant child, his own childhood and the life of the spirit in nature. This is contrasted with the sound of the 'redbreast' at the end of the poem. Here the small bird is also associated with winter cold and snow. But this bird is heard in the daylight and is associated with the child and his experience of Nature.

As the peace disturbs the poet's thinking he focuses on the activity of the fire. Even here there is little movement as the 'thin blue flame' that 'lies' on the 'low burnt fire' 'quivers not'. While the flame of the fire is unmoving there is another 'film' that not only moves but also connects with his own unquiet soul. This fluttering 'sole unquiet thing' is taken up in the second stanza as the 'fluttering stranger' which Coleridge recalls watching and contemplating as a child. This 'stranger', Coleridge recollects, allowed him to dream of his 'sweet birthplace', to sleep and dream and to search for the 'stranger's face'. Coleridge contrasts his own childhood searching for this 'fluttering stranger' with the ease with which his own son will find it because he is being brought up in the country and close to nature.

There are strong contrasting images of childhood in the poem. Images of the poet's childhood, which was largely spent in London, are contrasted with the images of the childhood which the child is experiencing. The contrast is further accentuated by the poet's recollections of how as a child he dreamed of his 'sweet birthplace'. The negative side of the city childhood is captured in images of the 'stern preceptor's face', the 'mock study', the 'swimming book' and the 'great city' with its 'cloisters dim'. This evokes a sense of all childhood pleasures being suppressed, and the knowledge contained in the book being devoid of the sensual experience of his early childhood. The contrast with this earlier period is contained in the images of his later childhood dreams. These include the music of the 'bells' of the 'old church-tower' which he describes as ringing so 'sweetly' that they 'stirred' and 'haunted' him 'with a wild pleasure', contrasting with the attempt to tame him in the school room. These sounds also foreshadowed the knowledge of the inner life of man and the universe that was yet to come.

The poet's unhappy and brooding childhood is further depicted through the image of snatching 'a hasty glance' through the 'door half-opened' to see beyond the classroom which was so oppressing his spirit. The contrasting childhoods are established through the images of his son who will be able to 'wander like a breeze'. The freedom and lack of constraint implied in this image is reinforced in the listing of the places in nature in which the boy will be able to wander — 'lakes and shores and mountain crags'. Importantly, there is a contrast in the poet's childhood searchings for the 'fluttering stranger' and his own son's opportunities to 'see and hear' the evidence of the 'eternal language' and to allow his own spirit to be moulded by the 'Great Universal Teacher'.

The image of the sleeping child pervades the poem. It is an image of innocence and gentleness. The 'gentle breathings' are effectively the only sounds in the 'deep calm' of this moment. They are connected to the only other sound in the moment, which is the cry of the young owl. The poet, drawn back from his musings to gazing at the child, expresses his intense emotions at the sight. The image of the 'babe so beautiful' 'thrills' him and fills him with 'tender gladness' as he realises the opportunities that are yet ahead for this child that were not available to him. The peacefulness of the sleeping child mirrors the peace and calm of the natural world to which the child is so closely connected.

The poem is written in four stanzas of blank verse. These stanzas are not regular but reflect the movement of the poet's thoughts and feelings. The first stanza, which establishes the domestic moment, is the longest. The second and third stanzas look back and then forward. The final stanza, which provides the conclusion to the argument that has emanated from the poet's reflections, is the shortest and has a firmness and certainty to it.

There is no use of rhyme in the poem although the repetition sometimes creates a sense of rhyme that reinforces particular ideas. For instance the repetition of 'sea, hill and wood' at the end of two adjacent lines reinforces these images of the natural world. Similarly, at the end of the poem the repetition of 'quietly' and 'quiet' returns the reader to the calm of the opening moments after the meditative journey that has disturbed thought. Other repeated patterns are used to emphasise the message of the poem. For instance the line: 'Himself in all, and all things in himself' reinforces Coleridge's idea about the presence of the 'Great Universal Teacher' whose presence is everywhere in nature and in humankind.

Coleridge, in rejecting rigid poetic forms, allows his ideas and moods to shape the poem in its conversational tone. To achieve this he makes use of a number of devices including direct address to the reader or listener and to the sleeping child. In the first stanza he draws the reader in to the moment with the words 'and hark again!', as if the reader is there with him listening to the sound of the young owl. Similarly, exclamations such as 'Tis calm indeed' and 'this populous village' assume that the reader is in the moment and sharing the feelings and seeing the gesture that indicates 'this' village. The address to the child comes in the third stanza, where the poet begins with the words 'Dear Babe' and continues to direct his thoughts to the child with words such as 'thou' and 'thee' which indicate not only his fondness for the child but a sense of reverence for the child's being.

Coleridge's conversation asserts his belief in the power of Nature to be the source of life for his child. The poem contrasts his own childhood experiences with those he imagines for his child. The presence of the spirit in nature is an important force in the education of the child and there is an uplifting sense of rejoicing as Coleridge asserts his belief that his child will know this from an early age.

Using the description and analysis in this study guide **and** your own reading of the poem make your own set of notes that answer these questions:

- **what** issues and ideas is the poem communicating?
- **what** feelings or emotions about these ideas are expressed?
- **how** are these expressed in the poetic form, features, techniques and devices?

This Lime-Tree Bower my Prison

This poem is usually published with a preface about the circumstances in which it was written. In June 1797 Coleridge had been expecting some friends to visit at his cottage. It is often assumed that these friends included Dorothy and William Wordsworth and Charles Lamb. His 'friend' Charles is mentioned within the poem three times by name although the other friends are not specifically identified. Just prior to their arrival Coleridge met with an accident which prevented him from undertaking any of the walks that he had expected to participate in with his friends. While they were out walking on one occasion he composed this poem.

Description

The following outline of the subject of the poem shows you how the poet's ideas are structured. You should use it to help you in your first reading of the poem and then explore and analyse how the poet expresses these ideas and feelings.

Stanza 1

| lines 1–5 | establish the poet's situation and his feelings of imprisonment in the lime-tree bower as his friends depart on the walk |
| | express his concern that he is being deprived of experiences that would enrich his memory in later years |

| lines 5–9 | express his despondency at the departure of his friends as they are able to walk in joy through the countryside to the place that he has described to them |
| | express his almost melodramatic fear that he may never see these friends again |

| lines 10–16 | describe the 'roaring dell' that his friends are walking to and re-create in the poet's imagination the physical characteristics of the place |

| lines 16–20 | express the poet's imaginative re-creation of what his friends will see as they reach the dell |
| | express the feeling of awe that this place arouses in those who view it |

Stanza 2

| lines 1–26 | express the poet's imaginative re-creation of their walk from the 'dell' as they move out into the light and look across the fields and up to the skies |

| lines 26–32 | continue the imaginative re-creation of his friends' responses to the countryside |

concentrate particularly on Charles, who has
'pined' after 'Nature' in his present state, which
the poet suggests has included many years
in the city and some considerable 'calamity'

lines 32–37 | address the elements of Nature: the sun, the
flowers, the clouds, the groves and the ocean
urge these elements to increase their powers
of healing

lines 37–43 | describe how Nature's healing power has
previously affected the poet
express the poet's wish that his friend should
be similarly touched by this experience
describe how this experience has been a
spiritual one in which the forces of Nature
have revealed to the poet the 'Almighty Spirit'

Stanza 3

lines 43–45 | establish a change of mood as the poet
expresses his sudden feeling of joy and
empathy with his friends

lines 45–47 | show the poet's changed attitude to his
imprisonment by his new-found description
of the lime-tree bower as 'little'
express the poet's sense that the bower has
not imprisoned his thoughts and feelings as
he has gazed at his surroundings

lines 47–51 | describe the foliage that the poet has been
looking at and the way that the sunlight has
played on the leaves and how the poet has
'loved' to watch this play of light and shade

lines 51–56 | describe the walnut tree and elms and the
'ancient ivy' which is climbing their trunks

	continue the sense of light and shade and give a depth to this with the contrasts of blackness and gleaming 'twilight'
lines 56–59	introduce the bat, swallow and bee, bringing sound and movement to the picture of nature
lines 59–64	draw a lesson out of the poet's experience of Nature
	articulate his perception of the constancy of Nature to the 'wise and pure'
lines 64–67	speculate that there are sometimes advantages in being deprived of some experiences, as the soul can then be uplifted through *imagining* those things not directly experienced
lines 68–76	describe how the poet has observed the 'last rook' winging its way home, and this bird connects him with his friend
	show the poet's assumption that as this bird flies into the fading light of the sun, not only he, but also his friend Charles, has observed it
	articulate the poet's belief that the bird has brought a 'charm' for Charles whom he recalls as one who is in tune with 'Life'

Analysis

The poem is addressed initially to the bower where he must remain as his departing friends leave him for their rambles. Alone in his garden bower, or arbour, he imagines the journey that they are taking and reflects on his own situation. He records the ways in which his feelings and attitudes change as he imagines the journey that the friends are taking. As the poem progresses he addresses the friends and, in particular, Charles (Lamb) with whom he is able to empathise very closely.

The main images of this poem include images of Nature and the imagination. The images of the natural world predominate and they are, in essence, images of both darkness and light. The image of the 'lime-tree bower' is established initially as a prison, and later as simply 'little'. It is nevertheless an image of enclosure that forces the poet to look inwards and to become introspective. In this state he is able to see beauty even in the bower.

The images of the natural world include those that Coleridge visualises as his friends go on their ramble. Initially these are images of a 'springy heath' and 'hill top edge' that suggest a joyful activity. The next images are those concerned with the descent into the depths of the 'dell'. Here there is a canopy as the hollow is 'o'erwooded, narrow, deep'. There is only 'speckled' sunlight in this part of the walk. The image of the ash tree with its 'slim trunk', 'unsunn'd and damp', and the waterfall whose movement causes the leaves on the ash to 'tremble' is set against the 'dark green file of long lank weeds'. These images mirror the mood of the poet, who is sinking into a deep despondency.

The change in the next stanza also mirrors the poet's changing mood. The images here include those of light and openness with the 'hilly fields and meadows' and the 'sea' and a ship with its sails furled between the two islands. This openness, the 'wide wide Heaven', is reflected in the changing attitude of the poet to what he is missing and his capacity to empathise with what the walk means to his friend, Charles. The images of light at this point are magnified with reference to the 'glorious' setting sun as a 'sinking orb' whose light has the power to heal his friend. The poet suggests that this vision comes in such 'hues as veil the Almighty Spirit'. This openness in his imaginings of his friend's ramblings is further transformed into sights that are 'richly ting'd' and have a 'deep radiance'. The trees now 'gleam' with a 'lighter hue' and dapple the 'sunshine'.

Nature is personified, or at least given powers that are spiritual. Nature, the spirit, is omnipresent. There is no 'plot so narrow' or 'waste so vacant' that Nature is not present there. The Spirit of Nature does not 'desert' those who are 'wise and pure'. Nature uses all its powers to ensure that 'the heart' is kept aware of 'Love and Beauty'.

The poem has three stanzas. They reflect the movement of the poet's moods and his meditations. The first stanza is concerned with the feeling that he has of being imprisoned in the bower while his friends are free to roam to the places which he has described to them. The poet's mood descends with the imagined journey of the walkers into the dell.

The second stanza deals with the imagined emergence of the friends from the dell and into the open meadows. Here the mood begins to lift as the poet imagines the joy that his friend Charles will be getting from this experience. The presence of the 'Almighty spirit' also helps to redirect his feelings to a more positive note.

In the final stanza the mood stays elevated and expands as the light seems to spread over the world. It is in this stanza that he achieves the revelation of the truth about Nature and its omnipresence and omnipotence — It is everywhere, with unlimited power and influence. Here too, the poet comes to terms with the notion that it is sometimes a good thing 'to be bereft of promis'd good' because this helps to 'lift the soul' and enables us to 'contemplate with lively joy the joys we cannot share'. This capacity for empathising with the experience of others is central to the message of this poem.

This conversation poem shows Coleridge asserting the healing power of Nature. The poem also demonstrates Coleridge's belief in the Imagination and its capacity to bring joy. As he journeys in his mind along the same walk that his friends are undertaking he communicates to the reader the sense of the powerful presence of the natural world. This confidence emerges at the end of the poem and reinvigorates his thinking about his situation.

 Using the description and analysis in this study guide **and** your own reading of the poem make your own set of notes that answer these questions:

- **what** issues and ideas is the poem communicating?
- **what** feelings or emotions about these ideas are expressed?
- **how** are these expressed in the poetic form, features, techniques and devices?

The Aeolian Harp

This poem was composed at Clevedon in Somersetshire. It is addressed to Sara Coleridge. Aeolus, in Greek mythology, was the son of Poseidon who became a friend of the gods as a result of his piety and justice. He was thought to have invented sails for ships, and he was given the task of being the guardian of the winds by Zeus. He later became the father of the winds and in Roman mythology was thought to be the god of the winds. He lived on the island of Lipara and was thought to keep the winds tied up in deep caverns and caves on the island.

The term Aeolian Harp was used to describe a musical instrument, often also called a lyre. It consisted of a box, over which were stretched strings of silk or fine gut, tuned in unison, on which the wind would produce tones with audible harmonics of a mingled and distant sweetness. Aeolian harps were commonly placed within open windows in much the same way in which we might today hang wind chimes.

Description

The following outline of the subject of the poem shows you how the poet's ideas are structured. You should use it to help you in your first reading of the poem and then explore and analyse how the poet expresses these ideas and feelings.

Stanza 1

lines 1–9 | address Sara, who is sitting beside the poet with her cheek pressed against his arm in the 'cot' (cottage) which is covered with jasmine and myrtle
describe the flowers as symbols of 'Innocence and Love'
establish that the two people are sitting watching the sunset and the approaching evening as the star, which is the symbol of 'Wisdom', appears in the sky from which the light is slowly fading

lines 9–12 | express the poet's delight at the situation and at the sensuousness of the 'scents' and the 'silence'

Stanza 2

lines 12–17 | show the poet drawing Sara's attention to the sound of the 'Lute' in the casement window
describe how the wind strikes its strings to produce sounds that remind him of a 'coy maid' who is 'half yielding to her lover'

lines 17–25 | liken the sounds made by the harp to that made by 'Elfins' as they are preparing to make a voyage on 'gentle gales' moving on 'untam'd wings'

lines 26–29 | express the poet's joy at the oneness of Nature
suggest that the soul meets in this union of the senses

lines 30–33 | express the thought that it is impossible not to love Nature when such union is brought into being

Stanza 3

lines 34–38 | address Sara
show the poet reminding her that when he stretches out on the slopes in the middle of the day, dozing in the sunlight, he is tranquilly musing 'upon tranquillity'

lines 39–43 | describe how he allows thoughts to pass across his mind and how they do so in the same way that the sounds are coming from the lute that they are presently hearing

Stanza 4

lines 44–48 | show the poet asking whether the whole of Nature is composed of diverse harps from which arise thoughts as the breeze sweeps over them
suggest that all thought might come from 'one intellectual breeze' that ultimately derives from God

Stanza 5

lines 49–52 | describe how the poet's gaze returns to Sara, whose look rebukes his fantastical musings, and he discerns the criticism that he should 'walk humbly' with God

lines 53–57	outline the poet's response as he tells her that her rebuke is well placed and he acknowledges that his 'shapings' have come from an 'unregenerate mind'
lines 58–60	remark that the poet may never think of the 'Incomprehensible' except with 'awe' and with 'praise', that is inwardly feeling
lines 61–64	assert that the need for this humility in his attitude to God comes from the healing power that God has used for him and the rewards that He has given to him in the form of 'peace', his precious cottage and the 'heart-honour'd Maid'

Analysis

There are four key patterns of images in this poem. These include the images of Sara, the 'Cot', Nature and the 'Incomprehensible'. Sara is described initially as 'pensive', with a 'soft cheek' that is leaning against the poet's arm. Following the poet's wild thoughts she is presented as having a 'more serious eye' which is capable of a 'mild reproof'. Coleridge addresses her as 'my Love', 'Beloved Woman' and 'Meek Daughter'. It is her capacity for humility that appears to bring him back from his wilder rambling thoughts. She does not reject his 'thoughts' but rather seeks to bring him back to walk humbly' with his God.

The Cot, or cottage, is 'o'ergrown' with the rambling plants of the natural world, particularly the 'white flower'd Jasmin' and the 'broad-leav'd Myrtle'. These plants are identified by the poet as symbolic of 'Innocence and Love' and the cottage itself seems to take on these qualities by the association with the plants.

The central image is of Nature. This image embraces the clouds which are depicted as 'rich with light' and the 'star of eve' which is 'serenely brilliant'. The 'scents' from the 'bean-field' and the sounds of silence in Nature are other important aspects of the imagery. This silence is contrasted with the sounds of the harp. The harp is 'caress'd' by the 'desultory breeze' and from this gentle stroking come the sounds that elicit such a deep response of the spirit. It has 'long sequacious notes' that 'sink and rise', and this sound is likened to the 'soft floating witchery of sound' that is made by 'Elfins'. The sound of the music from the harp intermingles with the sounds of Nature and this intermingling becomes an important image for the poet's own imagination. The image of the 'breeze' which 'warbles' combines the power of the senses so that there is 'A light in sound, a sound-like power in light'. It is this that allows the poet to 'muse' tranquilly 'upon tranquillity'.

The final pattern of images emerges from these musings. The sounds of the harp and the sounds of nature are so combined that he creates in his imagination a view 'of animated nature' consisting of 'organic harps diversely fram'd' and this leads him further to comprehend these thoughts as 'vain Philosophy's aye-babbling spring' and to realise that he cannot so simply account for the 'Incomprehensible' with these 'shapings of the unregenerate mind'. The final images return to the Cot and the peace and to Sara, after the realisation that he must not simply construct these wilder fancies but 'praise' his God 'with Faith that inly feels'.

The poem consists of five stanzas of unequal length that move with the poet's thoughts. The first stanza positions the poet and Sara within the grounds of the cottage. It moves from the stillness of the two people and the lushness of nature to the silence and stillness of the evening and the 'stilly murmur' of the 'distant Sea'. The mood of peace, calm and contentment is established here.

The mood changes a little in the next stanza as the sounds of the harp in the breeze waft into their consciousness. These sounds arouse the poet to listen attentively to the play of the sounds and to revel in the feelings that this music stirs within him.

The third stanza moves to another time, as the poet recalls the thoughts that he has 'at noon' when, lying in the sun with his eyes half closed, he is able to 'tranquil muse upon tranquility'. There is a restlessness and urgency to this stanza as the poet's mind is disturbed by 'idle flitting phantasies'.

The fourth stanza can be seen almost as a climax to the stirring of thought as the poet poses his question about the nature of all Nature. The last stanza returns the mood to a more tranquil and measured one. This is introduced by the word 'But' and the poet is brought back to earth after his flight of fancy.

In this conversation poem Coleridge once again shows his strong connection with the natural world and his belief in the power of this world. He also demonstrates his relationship with Sara and his need to reign in his fanciful wanderings of the spirit. This homely poem evokes empathy as Coleridge explores those deeper musings which sent him on a lifelong search for understanding.

 Activity

Using the description and analysis in this study guide **and** your own reading of the poem make your own set of notes that answer these questions:

- **what** issues and ideas is the poem communicating?
- **what** feelings or emotions about these ideas are expressed?
- **how** are these expressed in the poetic form, features, techniques and devices?

Kubla Khan

This poem is a fragment. It was first published at the request of Lord Byron. Coleridge himself did not see it as having any particular poetic merit, but allowed it to be published as a 'psychological curiosity'.

Description

The following outline of the subject of the poem shows you how the poet's ideas are structured. You should use it to help you in your first reading of the poem and then explore and analyse how the poet expresses these ideas and feelings.

━━━━━━━━ Stanza 1

lines 1–5	set the scene in Xanadu, the home of Kubla Khan, and the place through which the sacred river, Alph, runs
lines 6–11	describe the richness of the grounds surrounded by the 'walls and towers' and the detail of the gardens and forests all enclosed within these boundaries

━━━━━━━━ Stanza 2

lines 12–16	warn that this place is both beautiful and dangerous, at once 'romantic' and 'savage', 'holy' and 'haunted' present the image of the 'woman wailing for her demon lover' encapsulating the two opposing moods
lines 17–19	tell of how a fountain was forced from the compressed 'turmoil' of the chasm

lines 20–22	describe how, within the 'burst' of water from the fountain that was forced out of the cavern, there were also 'huge fragments' that were thrown about like 'hail' or 'grain' tossed in the air when it is being threshed
lines 23–24	describe the bursting of the fountain out of the ground as the birth of the sacred river
lines 25–28	describe the way the river wanders for five miles and how it moves through meadows and woods and caves until it reaches the ocean and how this arrival is tumultuous, but the ocean itself is 'lifeless'
lines 29–30	describe how Kubla Khan hears, in the midst of the 'tumult' of the river reaching the sea, the voices of some ancient beings who are predicting 'war'
lines 31–34	describe how the shadow of this 'dome of pleasure' floated 'midway' and made it possible to hear the 'mingled measure' that came from the fountain and from the caves
lines 35–36	comment on the ingenuity of this 'rare device' which allowed the warmth of the sun in the icy caves

Stanza 3

| lines 37–41 | introduce a character, an Abyssinian 'damsel' playing on her 'dulcimer', who appears to be unrelated to the pleasure dome |
| | recount how the poet recalls her from a vision or dream that he once had, and how he remembers her singing of Mount Abora |

lines 42–47	express the poet's desire to 'revive' her song within his memory so that he could 'build that dome in air' in his poetic music
lines 48–54	provide a warning that if the poet were able to rebuild this dome those who saw him would know that he had been bewitched

Analysis

The poem was written under somewhat strange circumstances. Coleridge was, at the time of its writing (1797), in poor health and had gone to stay at a lonely cottage in Exmoor. At this stage he was taking prescribed opiates for pain relief and after one dosage fell asleep as he was reading a travel book, Purchas's *Pilgrimmage*. The sentences which he was apparently reading prior to falling asleep are thought to be: 'Here the Khan Kubla commanded a palace to be built, and a stately garden thereunto. And thus ten miles of fertile ground were enclosed with a wall'.

The story, as told by Coleridge afterwards, was that he slept for about three hours and while he was sleeping he had vivid dreams during which he composed a poem of about two or three hundred lines. Coleridge asserted that the composition was unusual in that the poem did not merely appear as images but rather as 'things'. When he woke he had a very vivid recollection of the whole poem and began to set it down. He was, however, interrupted by a knock at the door and a visitor from Porlock, the neighbouring village, interrupted his writing. This visitor stayed for about an hour. When he left Coleridge found that he could remember nothing further of the composition and all that remained was some dim recollection of the general notion of the vision — 'all the rest had passed away like the images on the surface of a stream into which a stone has been cast'.

The additional bits which Coleridge recalled include these lines:

> Then all the charm
> Is broken — all that phantom-world so fair
> Vanishes, and a thousand circlets spread,
>
> And each mis-shape the other. Stay awhile,
> Poor youth! who scarcely dar'st lift up thine eyes —
> The stream will soon renew its smoothness, soon
> The visions will return! And lo, he stays,
> And soon the fragments dim of lovely forms
> Come trembling back, unite, and now once more
> The pool becomes a mirror.

The poem that does remain, however fragmentary, has its own coherence and is commonly considered to be complete within itself. This visionary fragment of a poem has an extraordinary poetic quality. It is a poem that seems to palpably demonstrate, not merely describe, the process of artistic or visionary creation. It is a poem that leaps off the page in trills of sound and movement.

Central to this poem is the character of Kubla Khan. Kubla Khan was, in reality, a thirteenth century Mongol emperor and Coleridge seems to be using this image of Khan's decree as a symbol of the omnipotent and perhaps omniscient artist. Khan's 'stately pleasure dome' seems to symbolise the powerful, intuitive, unconscious or preconscious urges that eventually erupt into the artistic creation.

The river, Alph, is central to the poem. The birth of the river, its journey through the countryside and chasms and its eventual submersion in the sea suggest the process of artistic creation. Coleridge seems to be suggesting both the richness and the turbulence of the process of creation through images such as 'fertile ground', 'incense-bearing tree', 'ceaseless turmoil seething' and 'swift half-intermitted burst'. The process is also marked by enormous energy seen in images such as 'forced', 'vaulted' and 'flung'. There is also an unevenness to the journey of the river, and therefore to the artistic creative process. At times, it 'meanders with a mazy motion' and at other times it 'sank in tumult'.

The pattern of images portrays the unfathomability of the process of artistic creation. This is suggested in images such as 'caverns measureless to man' and further echoed in the images which provide a paradoxical perspective, such as 'sunless sea' and 'lifeless ocean'. These contrasts further reinforce the incomprehensibility of the creative process. The images of fertility and fecundity are contrasted with images of destruction such as 'huge fragments' and 'rebounding hail'. The juxtaposition of the 'woman wailing for her demon lover' and the 'ancestral voices prophesying war' is a further contrast which emphasises the enigmatic quality of the poem's romantic notion of artistic creation.

The second section of the poem extends this idea. It is concerned with the recreation of the creative process. The image of the 'damsel with a dulcimer' is central to the notion of the imagination. Coleridge longs to re-create the image that has been given to him, and if he were able to do so, he would have tasted 'Paradise'. This connection of the spiritual and artistic sensibility underpins the ideas in this section of the poem. The 'damsel' is contrasted with the 'woman wailing' in the first section of the poem. This contrasting image again suggests the passionate and intuitive nature of the creative process.

Much of the force of this poem emanates from its strongly sensuous nature. This comes from the sounds and rhythms of the lines. Of particular significance is the ways in which the use of assonance and alliteration create the movement of the river. The use of alliteration involving nasal sounds helps to create the sense of slow movement in lines such as:

Five miles meandering with a mazy motion.

This is strongly contrasted with the alliteration of plosive and fricative sounds in lines such as:

A mighty fountain momently was forced:
Amid whose swift half-intermitted burst
Huge fragments vaulted like rebounding hail.

The play of long and short vowels in the lines accentuates these differing rhythms and moods. The interplay of the rhythm of the river and that of the maid's song is also evident in the line lengths that are shortened in the section that describes the 'damsel with a dulcimer'. Here the lines resemble a rhythmic pattern of a lyric, despite their basic narrative intention.

This poem challenges the reader to explore the highly compacted use of metaphor. While Coleridge himself has suggested that it is simply part of a longer poem, lost for all time, it is clear that there is a unity and completeness to this fragment. The focus on the creative process and its differing stages leaves the reader pondering long after the echoes of the dulcimer have died away. Like the poet himself, the reader retains the desire to re-create in the memory the song and the images of this remarkable poem.

 Activity

Using the description and analysis in this study guide **and** your own reading of the poem make your own set of notes that answer these questions:

- **what** issues and ideas is the poem communicating?
- **what** feelings or emotions about these ideas are expressed?
- **how** are these expressed in the poetic form, features, techniques and devices?

Writing about the poet

After studying each poem individually it is important that you consider the commonalities in the ideas, feelings and poetic features of the poems that you have studied by the one poet. You can do this by considering the following general questions about all the poems and writing notes in answer to the questions. Use a range of poems to justify your general statements.

- What subjects and ideas does the poet explore in the poetry?
- What emotions or feelings does the poet express in the poetry?
- What forms and structures does the poet commonly use?
- What techniques or devices does the poet commonly use to encapsulate these ideas and feelings?

You should then write an essay such as the following that deals with the poems of this poet in a general way:

- 'Coleridge's poetry reveals his passionate preoccupation with nature and the imagination.' How does the poetry reveal this?

In answering this question you need to:

- define what you mean by 'passionate preoccupation'
- define what you mean by 'nature and the imagination'
- identify the poetric structures and devices that 'reveal' this
- select two poems that allow you to evaluate the truth of the statement
- develop an argument that either supports, negates or qualifies the statement.

Section

4

Robert Frost

Introduction

Robert Frost was born in San Francisco in 1874. His father died when he was young and he then moved to the New England area. He was educated at Dartmouth College and at Harvard. He farmed in New Hampshire, worked in the mills in Massachusetts and then as an editor and as a teacher. He thereafter spent some time in London before his writings were eventually recognised. He collected numerous prizes and achieved wide public acclaim as one of America's foremost poets of the age. He read 'The Gift Outright' (written in 1942) at President Kennedy's inauguration and died in 1963.

Frost is often described as the nearest that America could come to establishing a poet laureate. He had a public profile that was derived in part from his image as a plain-talking, down-to-earth American citizen and, in part, from the way in which he made himself available to the public so that his image could be constantly reinforced. However, there were some critics who believed that he was selling literature short, particularly poetry, by adopting the particular public stance that he did. Frost's biographer, Lawrance Thompson, portrays Frost not as the lovable and loyal American, but rather as the conniving and manipulating public relations expert who knew how to promote his image and ingratiate himself with those in positions of power.

Regardless of the reputation of the man, his poetry is powerful in that it presents Frost's attempt to take traditional metrical forms and to manipulate these to allow for the incorporation of colloquial speech patterns. Frost himself says of poetry that 'the living part of a poem is the intonation entangled somehow in the syntax, idiom and meaning of a sentence. It is only there for those who have heard it previously in conversation.' This has the effect of making the poetry sound 'natural', as if you have caught the poet thinking out loud.

'Out, Out —'

This poem is a dramatic monologue and is written in one stanza. The title of the poem alludes to words spoken by Macbeth in Shakespeare's play. Macbeth has just learned of the death of his wife and as his whole life seems to collapse around him he speaks of what might have been and of the significance of life itself. In the speech he says:

> Tomorrow, and tomorrow, and tomorrow
> Creeps in this petty pace from day to day
> To the last syllable of recorded time;
> And all our yesterdays have lighted fools
> The way to dusty death. Out, out, brief candle,
> Life's but a walking shadow, a poor player
> That struts and frets his hour upon the stage
> And then is heard no more. It is a tale
> Told by an idiot, full of sound and fury
> Signifying nothing.

This speech is concerned with the notion that life is a fleeting thing that can be snuffed out as quickly as a candle and that thereafter the person is forgotten as others get on with their lives. This allusion to the words of Macbeth reinforces Frost's message in the poem.

Description

The following outline of the subject of the poem shows you how the poet's ideas are structured. You should use it to help you in your first reading of the poem and then explore and analyse how the poet expresses these ideas and feelings.

lines 1–3	present the image of the noise and action of the buzz saw which cuts timber into lengths that are small enough to fit in stoves, dropping sawdust on the ground as it does so
lines 4–6	put the sawmill into perspective of the landscape with the mountain ranges of Vermont behind it
lines 7–8	describe the noise and activity of the saw and the way that its sound changes according to the lightness or heaviness of the timber being cut
lines 9–12	comment that nothing had happened all day as the saw went on with its work articulate the poet's wish they had called it a day and ceased work, giving the boy an extra half hour off from work so that he could use the time in the way that boys do when they are released early from work
lines 13–14	describe how the boy's sister stood next to them telling them that 'supper' was ready
lines 14–17	describe how the saw seemed to understand what the word supper meant and leapt out of the boy's hand comment that the saw, at least, seemed to leap out, although the boy must have done something to contribute to this

lines 17–22	comment with dire understatement how the boy first laughed regretfully and held up the hand, partly in appeal and partly as if trying to save the lifeblood from spilling from the limb
lines 22–25	comment how the boy realised what had happened; even though he was a boy, he was doing man's work, and could see that the situation was hopeless
lines 25–27	articulate the boy's voice calling to his sister not to let the doctor cut off the hand comment that the hand was already severed beyond repair
lines 28–29	describe how the doctor anaesthetised the boy so that the breath simply 'puffed his lips'
lines 30–33	depict the suddenness of the death as the person watching for his pulse signals that it has faded presents the sense of disbelief as they listen to his heart which has stopped beating indicate the decision not to continue with the medical procedure since signs of life have gone
lines 33–34	comment ironically that those who were still living then went back to their own affairs

Analysis

The main image is that of the saw which dominates the poem. It is constructed primarily through the use of metaphor which personifies the saw. This personification also captures the saw as an aggressive and uncaring creature of great power. Words such as 'snarled' and 'rattled', which are repeated, reinforce this image. The physical and mental power of the saw is captured in the word 'leaped' and in the phrase 'to prove saws knew what supper meant'. This power is used to take away the life of the boy in that swift moment in which it 'leaped out at the boy's hand'.

The image of the hand is closely associated with the saw image. The saw is described as leaping at the hand, but this is counterpointed with the poet's comment that the boy 'must have given the hand'. The image of the hand is established primarily through the repetition of the word itself. The repetitions include those in the poet's narration — 'holding up the hand'; in the poet's comments — 'But the hand!' and 'But the hand was gone already'; and in the voice of the boy himself — 'Don't let him cut my hand off'. This lack of adornment of the word highlights the starkness of the situation and makes the image more powerful.

The power of the saw is contrasted with the innocence of the young boy. The first image of this youth is established in the comment of the poet that the young boy craves time 'saved from work'. This is reinforced by the image of the 'child at heart' and the 'big boy' who was 'doing a man's work'. The innocence of the boy is further established with the image of his 'rueful laugh'. This oxymoron brings together the idea of sorrow ('rue') and joy ('laughter') and indicates the swiftness with which the boy's understanding of the seriousness of the incident is coming upon him. This is further reinforced by the sound of the boy's voice, which contains a plea that is at once childlike and at the same time demonstrates his newly acquired adult understanding:

> ... Don't let him cut my hand off —
> The doctor, when he comes. Don't let him, sister!'

The final image of the boy is captured in the 'dark of ether' and the surprise as his 'breath' and his 'heart' are extinguished.

The suddenness and unexpectedness of the death also catches the doctor and those assisting him by surprise. This is starkly presented in the poem. The death is presented in a single line:

Little — less — nothing! — and that ended it.

The simplicity of this echoes the words in Shakespeare's play *Macbeth*, from which the title is derived. In the poem the ideas are reinforced by the contrasting image of disbelief in those observing the incident and the poet's comment that 'No one believed'. The anonymity of the 'watcher' and the 'doctor' further emphasises the notion of the fragility of life. The final line cements this idea as the others 'since they were not the one dead' get on with their own lives and 'their affairs'.

The other key contrasting image is that of the sister. She comes with the announcement of 'supper', an image of the nurturing female that is continued as the boy appeals to her as the full realisation of the situation dawns upon him. The presence of the sister carrying out this adult role of feeding the men standing 'beside them in her apron' suggests both the innocence of the young child but, like the boy, the assumption of the adult role.

Set against these images are those of the landscape — the 'five mountain ranges', the 'sunset' and the view 'far into Vermont'. The sense of vastness that these images create dwarfs the incident and its importance. There is a tension created between these elements. The loss of life appears to be diminished by the landscape in which it occurs. And yet there is a sense in which the loss of this innocent life represents a vast waste.

This poem is a single stanza which moves with the mood of

the events. The focus moves from the saw to the landscape, back to the saw and then to the boy, his sister and the saw again. The focus then moves into the hand and the activity that surrounds the attempt to repair the damage done to the hand by the saw. The final image of the dead boy is juxtaposed with the life that must go on for those who are left. The rhythm of the poem echoes this movement.

Frost does not use a regular rhyme pattern in this poem. Rather, he plays with the sounds of words, bringing some lines close together with a half rhyme, as in 'count' and 'Vermont' and 'load' and 'said', or a repetition of the word 'hand' at the end of lines. This reinforces the image of the hand that has been severed and is now impotent and about to be followed by the death of the boy.

This poem contains a powerful message in its simple diction and sentence structure. The bareness of the words creates a kind of tension with the magnitude of the message. Sentences such as 'But the hand was gone already' and 'No more to build on there' show the power of the ideas conveyed in the simplest language structures. Similarly, the intrusion of comments by the poet into the narrative create a sense of immediateness and urgency. These comments are quite colloquial and draw the reader in almost as if he or she were present in the moment. Examples of this include 'So' and 'Call it a day, I wish they might have said'.

As Frost presents this dramatic moment in verse the reader cannot help but be shocked. The connection with Macbeth's lines about the death of Lady Macbeth seem to give the poem a bitter reference point as it applies to the death of the young, innocent child who has been co-opted into man's work. The pathos of the moment is exacerbated by the actions of the other adults who return to their tasks after the expiration of the boy's last breath.

ctivity | Using the description and analysis in this study guide **and** your own reading of the poem make your own set of notes that answer these questions:

- **what** issues and ideas is the poem communicating?
- **what** feelings or emotions about these ideas are expressed?
- **how** are these expressed in the poetic form, features, techniques and devices?

Fire and Ice

This is a short poem of nine lines. It appears to be simple but like so many of Frost's poems, it deals with a profound notion.

Description

The following outline of the subject of the poem shows you how the poet's ideas are structured. You should use it to help you in your first reading of the poem and then explore and analyse how the poet expresses these ideas and feelings.

lines 1–2	begin with a comparative statement, contrasting the view of those who believe that the world will end 'in fire' with those who say it will end 'in ice'
lines 3–4	express the poet's preference for the view of 'fire', which he connects with 'desire'
lines 5–9	comment ironically that if the world were to end twice there would be a case for using ice because it is so connected with hate

Analysis

The idea of passion and desire is established through the image of fire. This image suggests a warmth and yet a destructive capacity. The opposite ideas are reinforced through the sound patterns, particularly the use of devices such as alliteration — 'favour fire'. The idea of hatred is captured in the image of ice. This image suggests a frozenness and yet a destructive capacity.

The notion of destruction is established in the opening lines of the poem with the image of the end of the world. Initially this image seems almost matter-of-fact, but it develops sinister connotations as it becomes connected with ideas such as 'perish' and 'destruction'. Thus the initial notion of the world coming to an end is seen as likely to be caused by human agency and the source of this agency is located in human desire or human hate.

The initial thesis contrasts two different views of the end of the world. One is an apocalyptic explosive burnout that is often associated with religious notions of punishment for the sins and evils of the world. The other view is an evolutionary one which suggests that there will be another great ice age that will cause the ice caps that are currently confined to the north and south poles to spread over the earth. Frost twists this idea to show that both the passions of desire and hate can cause apocalyptic harm.

The presence of the poet in the poem is highlighted by the repetition of the first person singular pronoun, 'I'. This is juxtaposed with the notion of 'some say' that is repeated in the first two lines, strengthening the poet's view. The poet asserts his authority by referring to the fact that he has 'tasted of desire' and that he 'know[s] enough of hate' to 'hold' his particular view. What is perhaps surprising about his view is that he is essentially saying that it is desire that is more destructive than hate.

This poem uses a regular rhyming scheme. There are three rhyming word patterns in the poem: 'fire', 'ice' and 'hate'. The rhyme is tightly controlled so that the ideas associated with these three patterns are juxtaposed: a, b, a, a, b, c, b, c, b.

The two ideas of 'desire' and 'hate' are introduced in the opening two lines with the juxtaposition of the two images of 'fire' and 'ice' and are further juxtaposed in the next two parts of the poem. This division is signalled with the conjunction 'but' that sets up the contrast between the destructive power of fire and ice.

This apparently simple poem challenges the reader to consider the significance of these metaphors. The juxtaposition of the two opposing images in this rigid poetic form carries a sense of irony that is at once humorous and biting. The reader ultimately wants to side with the poet, and yet is faced with the consequences of such a choice.

 ctivity

Using the description and analysis in this study guide **and** your own reading of the poem make your own set of notes that answer these questions:

- **what** issues and ideas is the poem communicating?
- **what** feelings or emotions about these ideas are expressed?
- **how** are these expressed in the poetic form, features, techniques and devices?

Stopping by Woods

'Stopping by Woods' appears to be a simple poem within the tradition of pastoral poems describing the beauty of the landscape. But there is something a little darker in the poem. This poem draws upon more traditional poetic forms. There are four quatrain stanzas, with three of the lines in each stanza rhyming.

Description

The following outline of the subject of the poem shows you how the poet's ideas are structured. You should use it to help you in your first reading of the poem and then explore and analyse how the poet expresses these ideas and feelings.

Stanza 1

> establishes the poet travelling home through the snow as he stops by the woods confident that the owner of the woods lives in the village and will not see him stop here

Stanza 2

> shows the poet imagining what the horse must be thinking at his decision to stop so far away from a farmhouse, near the woods and the frozen lake, on such a cold, dark winter evening

Stanza 3

> describes the way the horse responds, shaking his bells, as if asking whether there is some mistake in their stopping there comments on the silence with the only other sound being that of the wind and snowflakes

Stanza 4

> describes the poet continuing his journey
> expressing his pleasure in the woods, his
> need to keep his promises and the long
> distance before he reaches his resting place

Analysis

The main image in this poem is of the woods. The woods are described as 'lovely, dark, and deep' as they 'fill up with snow'. They are also silent, with the only sound being the 'sweep/Of easy wind and downy flake'. There is a peacefulness about these woods because of their stillness and their distance from human habitation. But there is also an air of mystery that is expressed in the image of the 'darkest evening of the year'. The mystery is indicated in the opening lines which suggest that the woods are owned by someone who is not present and may perhaps not allow the poet to stop where he is.

The silence of the woods is contrasted with the presence of the horse. The poet describes the horse using a term of endearment, 'my little horse', and we see that there is an affectionate relationship between the poet and this animal. The relationship is so close that the poet is able to speculate as to what the horse might be thinking:

> My little horse must think it queer
> To stop without a farmhouse near.

Not only does he read the mind of the horse, but the horse is able to communicate with the man:

> He gives his harness bells a shake
> To ask if there is some mistake.

The bond between man and animal seems to be stronger than the bond between human and human in this poem. This is suggested in the lines in which the poet notes that the owner of the woods will not see him 'stopping here/To watch his woods fill up with snow'. There is a suggestion of some imminent threat should the poet be seen by the owner of the woods.

The other mysterious part of the poem arises from the notion of the 'promises' that the poet has to keep. There is no real information in the poem about what these promises are and to whom they have been made. The reader can only speculate about this aspect, but what is clear is that these promises are strongly held and the poet feels compelled to keep them. There is also a sense that there is a long journey that must be made in order to keep the promises. The repetition of the line, 'And miles to go before I sleep' suggests a sense of compulsion and almost regret that this compulsion is driving him on from the peace and contentment of watching the snow falling in the woods.

This is a deceptively straightforward poem. Written in four quatrains, it seems to recount a single incident in the first person. The use of repetition gives the poem a feeling of almost childlike simplicity. This is reinforced by the simple diction and the interaction between human and animal that creates the ambience of a folk tale.

Contrasting with this is the tightly controlled rhyme scheme. There is one rhyming word in each stanza and this appears in the first, second and fourth line. The third line introduces a new sound in the last word, but in each stanza this sound becomes the rhyming word for the next stanza. Thus, in the first stanza the words 'know', 'though' and 'snow' rhyme. The other word is 'here' and it is the sound from this word that forms the basis of the rhyme in the next stanza where the rhyming words are 'queer', 'near' and 'year'. The new sound in the second stanza is 'lake' and it is the sound in this word that forms the basis of the rhyming pattern for the next stanza, in which we find the rhyme in words such as 'shake', 'mistake' and 'flake'. The unrhymed word in this stanza comes in the word 'sweep' and this sound is used in all the words in the final stanza as the pattern is broken, with the repetition of the line 'and miles to go before I sleep'.

There is a regular rhythmic pattern used throughout the stanzas based on the iambic beat. This gives a sense of steadiness and stillness as the poet recounts the incident.

This apparently simple poem has a depth that leaves the reader wondering long after the sound of the horse's bells have died away. The poem suggests that there is something more than a simple stop to admire the landscape on a winter's night, and yet the poem does not reveal more than this. It simply suggests and leaves the reader wondering.

Activity

Using the description and analysis in this study guide **and** your own reading of the poem make your own set of notes that answer these questions:

- **what** issues and ideas is the poem communicating?
- **what** feelings or emotions about these ideas are expressed?
- **how** are these expressed in the poetic form, features, techniques and devices?

The Road Not Taken

In this poem the poet uses the first person again to place himself within the context of the moral dilemma of the poem. This poem uses a more traditional verse form with four stanzas each of five lines.

Description

The following outline of the subject of the poem shows you how the poet's ideas are structured. You should use it to help you in your first reading of the poem and then explore and analyse how the poet expresses these ideas and feelings.

Stanza 1

sets the scene at a point in the woods where there is a fork in the road

establishes that there is a dilemma here as he cannot take both paths

describes how the poet stands and looks down one of the paths, attempting to see as far as he can to the curve where it disappears in the undergrowth

Stanza 2

tells the reader that the poet then took the other path which seemed just as good, although perhaps more enticing because it seemed to have had less wear than the first path

contrasts this idea with the comment that if the poet had to consider both paths it would appear that they were about the same

Stanza 3

continues the idea of the paths having equal wear and tear

comments that the poet had kept the other path for travelling down on another occasion

comments that it is unlikely that he would once again come back to this spot

Stanza 4

> comments that he will be telling this story
> with some regret in the future
> comments that there were two roads that
> went down divergent paths and his choice to
> take the one that seemed to be 'less traveled
> by' has 'made all the difference' to his life

Analysis

A key image in the poem is of the two roads. Both are described as 'fair'. The one not taken by the poet 'bent in the undergrowth' and like the other was covered in leaves 'no step had trodden black'. The one taken by the poet seemed to him 'grassy' and in need of 'wear'.

The persona of the poet has a strong presence in this poem. The poem is in one sense about the workings of the poet's mind. There are therefore many images of thinking and feeling. The poet tells of feeling 'sorry', of 'knowing' and having doubts and feelings of regret. This is contrasted with the certainty of the last line — 'And that has made all the difference.'

This poem is tightly structured, with five-line stanzas and a regular rhyme scheme. In each stanza there are two rhyming words. The first one links the first, third and fourth line, and the second links the second and fifth line. This scheme gives the impression of coming together and drifting apart.

The sense of time passing is strong in the poem. The poet begins in the simple past tense as if this were to be a recount of an event that has occurred and is over and done with. But there is an interplay of time past, present and in the future contained in the workings of the poem. This is particularly noticeable in the shift of verb tenses from the simple past to more complex deeper pasts — 'the passing there/had worn them about the same' — as well as projections into the future — 'I shall be telling this'. There is also a sense of a timeless present in the line 'knowing how way leads on to way' as if a universal truth has been uttered, and this provides the springboard for the final line.

This poem leaves the reader wondering, with the poet, about the path that the poet did not take. The poem seems to invite the reader to speculate what difference it would have made to the poet to have taken the other way. The poem does not reveal the consequences for the poet and this leaves the reader open to much speculation. Indeed the strength of this poem seems to lie in the things that remain unstated and simply hinted at.

Using the description and analysis in this study guide **and** your own reading of the poem make your own set of notes that answer these questions:

- **what** issues and ideas is the poem communicating?
- **what** feelings or emotions about these ideas are expressed?
- **how** are these expressed in the poetic form, features, techniques and devices?

Mending Wall

This poem is written in a single stanza. It is a dramatic monologue in which the author evokes the situation and incorporates the comments of his neighbour. The scene is a dividing wall or fence on a farm. The wall is a drystone construction which has stones and boulders piled on top of each other along the perimeter of the wall.

Description

The following outline of the subject of the poem shows you how the poet's ideas are structured. You should use it to help you in your first reading of the poem and then explore and analyse how the poet expresses these ideas and feelings.

lines 1–4 | comment that there is something that has no affection for walls and therefore seeks to swell the ground so that the stones on the upper part of the wall fall down and make gaps that allow people to pass through

lines 5–9 | note that hunters dismantle walls, but this is in addition to the type of destruction the poet is talking about in this poem
note that hunters pull down the stones to get at the rabbit and to please the dogs, which are yelping to indicate where the rabbit has disappeared
comment that the poet has to come along afterwards and repair the damage done

lines 9–11 | reiterate that the gaps the poet is talking about in this poem are quite different
comments that no one has seen or heard these being made, but in the spring they are simply there requiring mending

lines 12–14 | establish the poet as one of the farmers
indicate that when the wall needs mending he lets his neighbour know and they meet at an agreed time to collaborate in mending the wall that separates them

lines 15–16	describe how the two farmers keep to their own sides of the wall as they go about the task and each one picks up the boulders that have fallen to their side of the wall and replaces them
lines 17–20	establish that some of the boulders are long, while others are so round that it is hard to make them balance suggest that it is almost as if they use a spell on the boulders to make them stay in place describe how tough the work is and how their fingers are roughened with the task of handling the rocks
lines 21–22	comment that this is really just another kind of outdoors game with one person on each side
lines 23–24	comment that they really do not need the wall here explain that this side of the wall is an apple orchard and his neighbour's side is a pine forest
lines 25–26	recount his ironical comment to his neighbour that his apple trees will not get over the wall to eat his neighbour's pine cones
line 27	records his neighbour's response, which is the platitude that the mended wall will mean that they can be 'good neighbours'
lines 28–31	comment that perhaps because it is spring, the poet has a mischievous thought and wonders if he could get his neighbour to question why walls help create good neighbours

pose the question that a wall is only necessary where there are cows, but there are no cows on their farms

lines 32–36 | comment that he would like to ask his neighbour what is being walled in or out, and who might be offended by the wall, because something does want this wall down

lines 36–38 | comment that he could suggest that it is elves that want the wall down, but it isn't really elves and anyway he would want the neighbour to say that himself

lines 38–40 | comment that he is watching the neighbour bring stones now to the wall looking like an old armed savage man

lines 41–42 | comment that the neighbour seems to move 'in darkness' that is not only a literal darkness, but also the darkness of lack of understanding

lines 43–45 | comment that his neighbour is caught in the tradition that his father established and that he likes the thought of this tradition so much that he repeats his earlier statement that 'Good fences make good neighbours'

Analysis

The main image in this poem is that of the wall. Frost builds up this image with a complex interplay of descriptions. The wall is manipulated by forces beyond its control. These forces are both human and non-human. There is the force from the 'frozen-ground-swell' that 'spills the upper boulders' and the 'work of hunters'. The mending of the wall is carried out by the two neighbours. The wall is seen as a barrier or boundary that is 'set between' them. This boundary, however, opens up with gaps that allow 'two to pass abreast'. The wall takes on a kind of non-natural or magical ambience. Its deterioration seems to happen without any observers and it is mended using a 'spell' to keep some of the repositioned boulders in place. This notion of the non-natural wall is highlighted further with the mention of the 'elves' and the 'old-stone savage armed'.

A key set of images has to do with the stones that form the wall. These are described as 'boulders', 'stones', 'loaves', 'balls' and finally as making the neighbour look as if he is 'armed'. Handling the stones makes both men's fingers 'rough'. These stones are unfriendly and seem to have a mind of their own. The poet seems to be suggesting that they do not want to stay in the wall permanently. The stones are neatly contrasted with the apples and with the pine cones that lie on the ground on the neighbour's side of the fence.

The image of the neighbour in the poem is also important. The neighbour who grows a pine forest on his side of the wall is a man who clings to tradition. This is conveyed in the image of the 'spring mending-time' and the activity of 'walk[ing] the line' in order to mend the wall together. There is a ritualised action described in this mending of the wall: 'To each the boulders that have fallen to each'. While this is a collaborative activity it is also one that continues to divide the neighbour from the poet. The neighbour's clinging to his traditions and conventions is represented in the voice of the neighbour as he echoes the saying from his father: 'Good fences make good neighbours'. The repetition of this saying reinforces the image of this man stubbornly clinging to the past traditions. From the poet's point of view this man 'moves in darkness', as he refuses to 'go behind his father's saying'.

The poet's viewpoint is contrasted with that of the neighbour. The gently mocking tone of the whole poem reflects of the ridiculousness of the neighbour's point of view. The poet comments to the reader in a comical way that his own 'apple trees will never get across/And eat the cones' from his neighbour's pine trees.

The poet also comments on the kind of question that he would like to put to his neighbour: 'Why do they make good neighbours?'. He amplifies this question by presenting his viewpoint about the function of walls: 'walling in or walling out'. The poet is not only critical of the ritualised mending of the wall, but of the neighbour's manner of thinking, of the way that he justifies the action not by analysis of the present situation, but by reference to one of his father's beliefs. The poet describes him as 'mov[ing] in darkness'. This darkness is a darkness of the mind, an inability to see what is before his eyes.

This dramatic monologue invites the reader to enter into the situation of the wall-mending and in so doing to examine the rationale for erecting a wall between two human beings. More importantly, this poem challenges the reader to examine the kinds of pithy sayings which can be taken as wise or true: 'Good fences make good neighbours'. The poem suggests that such sayings need to be questioned and challenged rather than blithely accepted.

Activity

Using the description and analysis in this study guide **and** your own reading of the poem make your own set of notes that answer these questions:

- **what** issues and ideas is the poem communicating?
- **what** feelings or emotions about these ideas are expressed?
- **how** are these expressed in the poetic form, features, techniques and devices?

After Apple Picking

This poem is a dramatic monologue in which the poet addresses the reader. It is written in one stanza. It is set in autumn at the end of the apple-picking season and the poet is finished with the apple picking even if all the apples have not actually been picked.

Description

The following outline of the subject of the poem shows you how the poet's ideas are structured. You should use it to help you in your first reading of the poem and then explore and analyse how the poet expresses these ideas and feelings.

lines 1–5	set the scene and describe the ladder still standing beside a tree, a barrel that has not yet been filled and some apples still on the bough of a tree
lines 6–8	comment that the poet has had enough of picking apples, even if they are not all picked, and since he feels the approach of winter he is beginning to drowse off to sleep
lines 9–13	recall the strange experience of the morning when he skimmed ice from the water trough and looked through it at the frosty grass, and the ice melted and fell to pieces on the ground
lines 14–17	comment that even though he was about to fall asleep he knew what kind of dreams he would be about to have
lines 18–20	describe the dream of apples that are magnified so that both ends are clearly visible as are all the markings on their skin

lines 21–23	describe how his foot not only aches but he can feel the rung of the step ladder as if it were still pressing on his instep, and he can also feel the movement of the ladder as the boughs bend
lines 24–26	describe how the poet continues to hear the sound of the rumble as the apples are poured into the cellar bin
lines 27–29	comment that the poet has had 'too much' apple picking and that he is tired out with the harvest of the apples that he had so wished for
lines 30–32	describe the extent of the apple harvest — 'ten thousand thousand' apples, all needing to be hand picked and handled into the bins
lines 33–36	point out that any apples that were dropped, regardless of whether they were obviously damaged, were relegated to the cider bin because they were worthless
lines 37–42	return to the notion of his approaching sleep and what will obviously disturb it
question whether it is the same kind of hibernating sleep that the woodchuck takes, or simply a 'human sleep' that is the result of sheer exhaustion

Analysis

The first image is that of the ladder which is described as 'long' and 'two-pointed' and standing up 'sticking through a tree/ Toward heaven'. This establishes the apple picking context that is developed through a series of images that provide further layers of meaning. The 'barrel' is standing beside the ladder and it is either empty or only partially filled.

The notion of approaching winter is established in the image of 'essence of winter sleep' which suggests the core of the cold season as the need to curl up and sleep in order to restore oneself. The idea of the essence is picked up in the 'scent of apples' and the 'drowsing off'. The image of sleep is magnified as other layers of meaning are added. The notion of rubbing the eyes, falling asleep, and dreaming of aspects of the apple picking are all layered over the original image of picking apples.

The image of the 'pane of glass' — the ice that was 'skimmed' from the 'drinking trough' — is a potent image in the poem. The fragility of the ice as it falls to the ground is to mirror the fragility of the dreaming images that will come and go for the poet as he withdraws from the apple picking. It comes to represent the relationship between the reality and the non-reality of the apple picking.

The poet withdraws from the reality of the apple picking, having had sufficient of this experience. But the experience of apple picking is not yet over and he relives the experiences in his imagination. What is significant is that this reliving occurs as a sensuous experience. It has a strong visual element — the apples are 'magnified' and their appearance is obvious in every detail, with 'every fleck of russet showing clear'. There is a strong sense of the tactile in the images of the 'instep arch' that 'keeps the ache' and that registers the 'pressure of the ladder-round', as well as feeling 'the ladder sway as the boughs bend'. There is a strong sense of the auditory in images such as the 'rumbling sound' of the apples tumbling into the 'cellar bin'.

In this dramatic monolgue the poet plays with line length and with rhyme to communicate the mood and message. He intersperses long and short lines, with the shorter lines creating a sense of the interruption to the apple picking even though the job might not be entirely done. Sometimes the rhyme of the short and long lines accentuates this. For instance, in the first six lines of the poem, he rhymes the first and fourth lines, the fifth and sixth lines and the second and third lines. The second line is also a short line and the rhyme in this and the next line — 'still' and 'fill' — creates the sense of the interruption to the apple picking. This rhyming pattern is continued throughout the poem with some variations. For instance, in lines fourteen, fifteen and sixteen, the rhyming words are 'well', 'fell' and 'tell'. There are two short lines in this sequence with the longer line in the middle.

Frost's dramatic monologue takes the reader into the situation of the apple picking and the sense of exhaustion that the poet has experienced. The richness of the imagery and the flow of the lines allow the reader to empathise with the poet's situation as he turns to his well-earned rest.

Activity

Using the description and analysis in this study guide **and** your own reading of the poem make your own set of notes that answer these questions:

- **what** issues and ideas is the poem communicating?
- **what** feelings or emotions about these ideas are expressed?
- **how** are these expressed in the poetic form, features, techniques and devices?

Writing about the poet

After studying each poem individually it is important that you consider the commonalities in the ideas, feelings and poetic features of the poems that you have studied by the one poet. You can do this by considering the following general questions about all the poems and writing notes in answer to the questions using a range of poems to justify your general statements.

- What subjects and ideas does the poet explore in the poetry?
- What emotions or feelings does the poet express in the poetry?
- What forms and structures does the poet commonly use?
- What techniques or devices does the poet commonly use to encapsulate these ideas and feelings?

You should then write an essay such as the following that deals with the poems of this poet in a general way:

- 'In Frost's poetry we commonly find a depth of thought in a simple poetic form.' To what extent is this true of the poems that you have studied?

In answering this question you need to:

- define what you mean by 'depth of thought'
- define what you mean by 'simple poetic form'
- select two or three poems that allow you to evaluate the truth of the statement
- develop an argument that evaluates the veracity of the statement.

Robert Gray

Introduction

Robert Gray is a contemporary Australian poet living and working in Sydney. He was born in Port Macquarie in 1945. His father had come from a well-to-do family in Sydney. He had, however, disgraced himself by dropping out of university; he failed to hold down any employment, engaged in drinking and gambling and was effectively banished to the north coast. Gray's mother was a local farm girl, who was uneducated in the way that the father had been. She was very religious. Gray describes their marriage as essentially unhappy except on a few occasions when his father turned on his charm.

Gray's formative years were filled with the light and vitality of the Australian bush and the tensions within the family. He locates the source of this tension in the father's capacity for verbal oppression. His adolescent years were particularly turbulent and rebellious. When turbulence erupted at home Gray enjoyed escaping into the bush. Gray left home and school at the age of seventeen without matriculating and spent time living on the fringes of society up and down the Queensland coast.

Gray did not begin writing poetry until after he left school. He sees poetry as giving access to feeling. He took a job as a cadet journalist on the local paper and there learned to use language more efficiently. He also met a landscape painter who has influenced his writing over the past thirty years. Gray has worked not only as a journalist and writer but also in jobs such as gardening and cleaning. He has also received many Literature Board grants to assist in his writing development.

His poems are deeply personal and reflect his experience of life. In several of the poems he recalls and relives the experiences of his days on the north coast of New South Wales and his travelling to and from Coffs Harbour.

Diptych

A diptych is a picture that contains two parts, each of which communicates a cohesive idea or image; both these separate parts taken together make up a whole image that communicates more than the simple sum of the two separate parts. The diptych was often placed like an open book above an altar. The two parts of this poem are focused on the poet's mother and father as separate human beings. Together the two parts communicate the poet's understanding of the different but complementary parts that the two parents played in the family.

Description

The following outline of the subject of the poem shows you how the poet's ideas are structured. You should use it to help you in your first reading of the poem and then explore and analyse how the poet expresses these ideas and feelings.

Part 1

lines 1–6 | introduce the mother
recount the mother's story of the father's late arrival home from the pub on one particular night and how she had lain awake waiting for him, knowing that if no one drove him, he would have to walk in his inebriated state

lines 7–13	tell that the father had previously driven his own car off the road and that a legend had developed of how he had ridden over the tops of the banana palms which had saved him from injury and how he had climbed out of the car and never driven again
lines 14–20	return to the particular night in which the mother was waiting and recount how she had dozed off to sleep fully clothed on the bed and woke later, with a foul taste in her mouth, aware at once that her husband was still not home, and how she had rushed outside, 'gagging', only to discover that she had bitten off the tail of a lizard, 'dragged through her lips'
lines 20–23	comment that the poet used to imagine the bitterness and the mother running outside 'to spit' and her standing there looking towards the town only to see that the lights were all out
lines 24–26	recount how his mother continued to look after the father, despite the fact that she was essentially uneducated and could be difficult to deal with, particularly at meal times
lines 27–28	explain the mother's behaviour in terms of the care that she took about things and that care was her only companion over this period
lines 29–33	describe her as being two different people, one 'harassed', the other 'calm' and it was this calm side that was aware of what needed to be done and guided her

lines 34–39 | describe how the mother's caring about her seedlings had given her the strength to force her neighbour's bull out of her garden using simply a broom
recount how she pushed the bull out slowly and step by step through the broken fence
recall that the poet was five at the time and that he kept calling to the mother to let the bull have 'a few old bloody flowers'

lines 40–45 | recount how the mother had tried to push the bull with the broom handle across his nose but the bull forced her back, and how, undeterred, she ducked behind some tomato stakes and then emerged and beat it with the broom handle and pushed the brushes into the bull's eyes, and eventually pushed it out

lines 45–48 | explain that the poet had stood 'in torment' watching on the sidelines, slapping a cord against the steps, rushing in to help and being repelled, and retiring to the sidelines to barrack

lines 48–50 | recount how, immediately after pushing the bull out, the mother set to tending the tiny seedlings that the bull had threatened to trample

Part 2

lines 51–52 | comment on the poet's father and the nature of his 'caring'
describe how the father cared that he not appear a 'drunkard' and sought to always ensure that 'his shoes were clean' to allay the appearance of an inebriate

lines 53–55	explain the father's definition of a drunkard as someone who had forgotten the 'mannerisms' that properly belonged to a gentleman since a gentleman was defined in terms of 'manner'
lines 55–58	describe his father as having 'perfect manners', 'of a kind' that were 'precise' and 'subsumed all of feeling'
lines 58–63	describe the kind of manners that his father was passionate about, including the brushing and doffing of a hat and the unfolding of a napkin after surveying those at the table comment how out of place this was in a hot town where most men sat without a shirt to eat their evening meal comment that the father was a 'university man' although he had not graduated, and this was more rare in those days
lines 63–66	comment that the poet now realises that his father was 'hopelessly melancholic' and that this was reflected in his face and physique
lines 67–69	descibe how his father was a lone drinker at the RSL club and how he would also drink alone in the sandhills, though wearing a carefully selected tie
lines 70–77	describe how he would look into the bedroom at his father when he was ill and home at nights and would see, in this 'gauzed verandah', the high dome of his skull as he was reading in bed surrounded by cigarette smoke

describe the way the light would shine through the mesh onto the plants in the garden and the insects that were attracted to the light and crawled near him, ignored by him

lines 77–79 | comment that he seemed content during these periods and that it was as if he had done all he could and was resigned to the situation

lines 80–84 | explain how he liked his bland food and the library books that he brought to his father
explain how his father gave instructions as to which books were to be brought from the library

lines 85–89 | note that his father only once seemed to actually enjoy something and that was being up in the bush, in the forests where the trees are tall and where he could 'feel at peace'
recall that the poet was 'impressed'

lines 89–90 | recall that on another occasion his father had asked that his ashes should not be put with the locals in the cemetery but taken somewhere else

lines 91–95 | explain how, when his father died, he went up to one of the hills which his father had named all those years ago, at the time of day that his father had mentioned, and that he found the sun 'strongly spiked' through the trees as it was on his father's Infantry badge
explain that he scattered the ashes there, seeing him 'reduced' in the grass that is blown by the wind and wet with the rain

lines 96–98	comment that he had by this stage come to accept his father, despite his 'callousness' to his mother
	note that his father had given him good advice and left him alone
	comment that by this stage he had come to think of most people as 'pathetic' and this made it easier to accept his father
lines 99–103	recount the scattering of his father's ashes and how, as he opened the can containing the ashes, the pocket knife slipped and slid sideways, cutting his hand
	tell how he dipped the wounded hand into the ashes which were like 'marble dust' and this action left him feeling that there was nothing more that needed to be said

Analysis

The poem presents a view of the poet's parents. It is almost as if by recalling the images of both parents he is able to come to terms with his feelings about them.

In the first section or panel of the poem the poet deals with images of his mother and her relationship with his father. There is a juxtaposition of the two different nights signalled in the images of 'one night' and 'this other night'. In the first night referred to the mother shows her compassion and understanding of the father and his inebriated state that would render him in need of assistance. This is contrasted with the second night in which she was 'reluctant' to go out looking for him. These contrasting images show the duality and ambivalence of the relationships between the parents and the difficulty of the poet in coming to terms with his own relationships.

There is a further juxtaposition of images as the poet recounts, in parentheses, the story of the father's drunken car accident and the mother's accident in biting the tail off a lizard that had crawled into her mouth. The father's story is told with a certain humour signalled in the phrase 'becoming legend' and the anti-climax of the accident from which the father had walked away 'most soberly polite'. The use of the metaphor 'rode/on the knocked-down banana palms' also adds to the humour of the situation suggesting a rodeo ride over the banana palms which grow on the side of the steep hills around the banana-growing areas of the mid north coast. This metaphor is extended to the car which 'reared high on a great raft of mutilated, sap-oozing fibre'. The effect is amplified by the rhythm of the lines which echo the movement of the car and the onomatopeic portmanteau word, 'sap-oozing'.

The mother's story is literally and metaphorically more bitter. In deciding to stay with the children while waiting for the return of her husband, the mother had fallen asleep while a small lizard had crept into her mouth. Her awakening to the 'foulest taste' is also climactic but there is not the same sense of humour here. The punctuation in these lines reinforces this bitter moment, with the distraction of the father's absence and the need 'to spit' out the vile taste that was clinging to her mouth. The movement of the mother in this anecdote is much more sharp and angular by comparison with the curving movements of the father's car crash, and the rhythm of the lines reinforces this, as do the harsher sounds in these lines.

The series of images that the poet uses to convey the sense of his mother reveals a woman who is both caring and hard. The poet suggests that her caring side was, in the final analyis, more powerful than the other side, and even that the other side was ultimately motivated by her 'care for things'. The image of the mother as one who 'only ever read the Women's Weekly' suggests a woman of that generation for whom education was not valued. The poet's comparison of this with her capacity for 'extending care', which he identifies as a philosophical position, allows the reader to see the mother in a larger context as he comes to terms with his relationship with her. Her care for her 'seedlings' he comes to realise was important for her.

The juxtposition of the image of the bull and the tiny seedlings with the mother in between creates a powerful picture of the two sides of the mother. In this anecdote he describes the way in which she uses the broom as a weapon against the bull to save the tiny seedlings. This picture is made more powerful by the detailed descriptions of the ways in which she used the broom, for instance, 'locked the broom handle straight-armed across its nose', 'beat it with the handle' and 'poked with the millet'. There is a sense of the resourcefulness of the woman as she makes use of every part of the broom.

There is also a wonderful juxtaposition of images associated with the actions of the mother and the bull. The verbs and verb groups emphasise this. The verbs that indicate the mother's actions include 'drive out', 'forced', 'locked the broom handle', 'pushed right back', 'ducked behind', 'beat', 'poked', 'had her way' and 'drove'. The verbs that indicate the bull's actions include 'trample', 'bellowing' and 'hooking'. This contrast gives a sense of the enormous power of the mother as she quells the bull and her frightened five-year-old son.

There is a further contrast in this anecdote with the actions of the boy — the young poet. Again this is reflected in the verbs. Those associated with the boy include 'calling', 'stood slapping', 'rushed', 'was quelled', 'repelled' and 'barracking'. The young boy's ambivalent feelings of admiration and fear are also juxtposed with the older poet's feelings as he retells the incident. The poet is able to comment on this from the distant perspective of his own adulthood. This commentary appears in the word 'No', in the reported speech of the child, as well as in the concluding statement, 'And all,/I saw, for those flimsy leaves'. This indicates the poet's realisation that as a young child he could not comprehend his mother's motivation in beating the bull away from the seedlings — 'small as mouse prints'.

The realisation that comes to the poet is contained in the image of the 'care for things'. This is presented in the metaphor of care as a 'companion' and in the simile of the reappearance of care 'like the edge of tidal water/ in salt flats'. These two disparate images are brought together in the use of the image of what the poet could 'see'. The use of verbs associated with watching and seeing takes on a bigger significance as the poet not only sees but comes to understand the significance of what he once saw. This is evident in the use of different tenses in lines such as:

> This care for things, I see, was her one real companion
> in those years.

and

> ... And all,
> I saw, for those little flimsy leaves ...

The contrast of the image of his mother with the image of his father is signalled in the opening word of the second section of the poem, 'Whereas'. This part of the poem also focuses on what the poet came to understand about his parents. This is communicated in phrases such as 'I see', and in the final line in which the poet reaches a situation of understanding from which he did not need to 'think of anything else to say'.

There is also a duality about the father's personality that has been hinted at in the anecdote of the car crash. This duality has to do with appearance and reality. For the father, appearance was focused on 'perfect manners'. The image of the father's manners, which 'had subsumed all of feeling', encapsulates the poet's understanding of his father. He presents this understanding not in key anecdotes as he does the mother, but rather as a running commentary on the father's qualities.

The outstanding quality that the son focuses on is his father's drinking. The poet describes the solitary nature of that drinking and the way in which the father sought to cover up his addiction to the outside world. The father's concern never to 'appear a drunkard' led to his determination to ensure that 'his shoes were clean'. The poet identifies the father's capacity to deny his addiction through his gentlemanly behaviours. The descriptions of these behaviours evoke pathos rather than humour. The images of doffing the hat and unfolding the napkin before dinner create a sense of a man living in another world. As the poet recounts this aspect he also comments on it by, for instance, comparing this behaviour with that of other men in the town who 'sat to eat of a hot evening without a shirt'. The juxtaposition of words such as 'to allow the meal' and 'to eat' reinforce this impression of the father.

The complex contrariness of the father is also presented in images such as 'the bitterness of every pleasure', 'hopelessly melancholic' and 'a university man/(though ungraduated)'. The image of the father with the 'carefully considered tie' getting drunk 'in the sandhills, watching the sea' further reinforces the impression of the complexity of this man.

The poet focuses much of his description of his father on the physical appearance and physique. There is precise description of his eyes, lips and 'long-boned face', as well as his 'high-domed skull'. This physical description contrasts with the description of his ashes as the poet takes them up into the hills. The poet describes the 'plastic, brick-sized box' which contrasts sharply with the value placed on 'manners' associated with the father when he was living. The description of the ashes in the simile 'like a mauvish-grey marble dust' seems to return the sense of dignity to the man who had once lived. The description of the hand that is 'pierced' and then used to scatter the ashes is a particularly powerful image of reconciliation.

The images of the father's bedroom, on the 'gauzed verandah', and the 'curdle of cigarette smoke' suggest that the father is akin to a caged animal and that the son has only a hazy view of him. This is reinforced by the images of the 'packed hydrangea-heads', the 'great ragged mass of insects' and the use of the simile of 'bees over a comb'. These images of unrest are juxtaposed with the images of the father's sense of contentment, as for instance, 'his bland ulcer patient food' and the 'library books'. However, underpinning this, his irritability still lurks and we hear this in the voice of the father himself as the poet quotes the instructions for the selection of the books.

These images are lifted by the one anecdote that is given a particular moment. The father speaks of the one thing that he enjoys — the peace in the hills. The poet stresses that this only happened 'once'. This image of peace becomes a strong symbol for the poet. Once again the poet records this in the father's own voice. This anecdote is extended to encompass the father's request that his ashes not be scattered with the locals. Once more there is the sense that the father sees himself as above or at least distant from the local community.

The image of peace is also juxtaposed with the image of war in his father's Infantry badge which featured a representation of the sun's rays. The poet experiences this 'strongly-spiked' sun when he goes into the hills to see for himself the place that his father has spoken of. This action seems to cement his acceptance of his father and 'his callousness' to the poet's mother.

This poem explores the poet's memories of each of his parents. The reader is presented with two clear portraits that show not only the particular qualities and characteristics of each but also the interconnectedness of the two. The diptych form emphasises the separateness of this married couple. In the final analysis the reader comes to see the poet's acceptance of each of his parents and their individual foibles in a compassionate way.

ctivity

Using the description and analysis in this study guide **and** your own reading of the poem make your own set of notes that answer these questions:

- **what** issues and ideas is the poem communicating?
- **what** feelings or emotions about these ideas are expressed?
- **how** are these expressed in the poetic form, features, techniques and devices?

The Meatworks

This poem is a monologue which describes the poet's feelings about the works and the people who lived there. It challenges the reader to confront the practice of slaughtering animals and eating meat.

Description

The following outline of the subject of the poem shows you how the poet's ideas are structured. You should use it to help you in your first reading of the poem and then explore and analyse how the poet expresses these ideas and feelings.

lines 1–6	comment on the workers at the meatworks describe how most of them worked out the back where the smell from the slaughtering sent the 'flies mad'
lines 7–9	contrast this with the work that the poet took — the lowest paid — making mince, but at least he was able to be away from the 'sloppy' yards where the animals bellowed
lines 9–11	comment that outside in the yards the fear that the pigs experienced caused them to 'mount one another' just prior to the slaughter
lines 11–19	describe how the poet stood all day pushing slabs of slaughtered meat into the mincing machine using a stick 'shaped into a penis'
lines 20–24	recount how the first time the poet had taken the stick to push the flesh into the mincer, it had slipped out of his hand into the machine which had tried to grind it for some time before 'shuddering' to a stop and fusing the electric circuit in the abbatoir
lines 26–27	comment wryly that because it was the first time he had done something wrong they couldn't sack him
lines 28–34	describe how after this event he was given the tasks, perhaps as a kind of warning or punishment, of carting the carcases of pigs into the cool room and hanging them up by their feet on hooks, and packing sausage mince into a skin that was like a 'long intestine'

lines 35–37	describe how the workers were given bags of meat to take home and how these were red plastic through which you could see the fat
lines 38–42	describe how the workers would attempt to wash themselves but how the blood seemed to get in around your nails
lines 43–46	describe how the poet would not take the meat and would walk home via the beach past the town
lines 47–49	recount how he would come to the beach and describe the mountains beyond the fibro houses of the town
lines 49–50	explain that the only employment available in the town was at the meatworks
lines 50–52	recount how his wife would come to meet him on the beach, carrying her sandals
lines 52–56	explain how he would use shell grit to scrub his hands and wash them in the icy waters of the surf
lines 56–59	explain the workers' view of the meatworks, comparing it to the burning of the bush and fertilising 'with rottenness' for money
lines 60–62	comment that they felt that there was a 'flaw' in this 'analogy', but they did not look at it at the time
line 63	identifies the flaw in the reasoning as the way that the pigs clung to each other

Analysis

This poem contains some of Gray's most potent images. The meatworks are described as the only place where there was employment in the town where the poet lived. There is juxtaposition of the notion of 'work' as employment and the 'Works' where the pigs are slaughtered. There is a subtle question as to what kind of work this actually is and this is picked up in the final comments of the poem as the poet reveals the 'flaw to the analogy'. The comparison that the poet and his wife made about 'working with meat' included the notion of killing something live and wild and 'fertilising with rottenness' in exchange for money, which is presented as something 'frail'. The flaw in this comparison, although felt by the poet at the time, was not faced — 'then'. This flaw was concerned with the pigs and their clinging to each other.

The images of the pigs permeates the poem, particularly the images of the live pigs. The dominant image is of their 'fear' — a feeling that is so strong that they seek to 'couple' in their 'last minute'. This image is repeated at the end of the poem in the phrase 'clinging onto each other'.

The most potent images are those of the dead pigs. The 'hot, fertilizer-thick, sticky stench of blood' is a powerfully sensuous image whose force is gained from the catalogue of adjectives that evoke strong connotations. The 'gutted pigs/white as swedes', the 'straight stick tails' and the 'snail-sheened flesh' are also powerful images of aspects of the dead pigs. The comparison with the natural world emphasises the killing of essentially innocent creatures.

The images of the dead pigs are further extended by the images of the mechanical works of the slaughterhouse. This is particularly evident in the mince-making that the poet settles for, despite its low pay. These images include the 'shaking metal box' which almost seems to have a life of its own. The 'shute' and 'spout' give it a surreal monster-like appearance and this impression is further reinforced by the image of the 'chomping, bloody mouth' which 'gnawed hysterically' on the stick which the poet has accidentally dropped into the mincer.

There is a strong contrast between the atmosphere of the meatworks and the natural world of the beach where the poet goes to be cleansed of his work. The image of the 'shell-grit' — the broken shells that have been naturally ground by the force of the waves — is neatly juxtaposed with the grinding of the flesh of the pigs, and this juxtaposition further reinforces the horrendous feeling of the slaughterhouse. The coldness of the water in which he is washing — 'icy ledges of the surf' — is further juxtaposed with the hot stench of the 'concrete gutters'.

The impersonal nature of the work is emphasised in the images of the other workers. None of them appear as anything other than 'they' or 'most of them'; and even when the poet 'fused every light in the shop', the authority figures are not even named — 'Too soon to sack me'. The workers also appear as 'We' in the two images of 'We got meat to take home' and 'We'd wash'. By contrast the poet identifies his feelings through the personal pronoun, 'I'; and we, the readers, come to realise that this work has had a profound effect on him, not only in the moment but also as he looks back from the distance of time.

This poem challenges the reader to confront a range of issues related to the killing and consumption of meat and the notion of work in a country town. The force of the poem comes from the narrative thread that runs throughout and the vibrant images of the pigs. The reader is presented with the picture of the pigs both alive and slaughtered and these images seem almost to leap off the page and soil the reader's hands. Ultimately, the non-questioning of the logic of the situation by the poet is presented to the reader as a challenge to be addressed.

ctivity

Using the description and analysis in this study guide **and** your own reading of the poem make your own set of notes that answer these questions:

- **what** issues and ideas is the poem communicating?
- **what** feelings or emotions about these ideas are expressed?
- **how** are these expressed in the poetic form, features, techniques and devices?

Late Ferry

This poem is written in quatrains. It appears on the surface to be a simple poem that describes the situation of a ferry on Sydney Harbour at night. But there are also some deeper ideas about our perception of the world.

Description

The following outline of the subject of the poem shows you how the poet's ideas are structured. You should use it to help you in your first reading of the poem and then explore and analyse how the poet expresses these ideas and feelings.

Stanza 1

> establishes that the poet is on the balcony watching the 'late ferry' leave and go up the 'huge dark harbour'

Stanza 2

> describes the ferry as it moves beyond the jetty; the poet listens to the sound of the palm trees making a noise like a brush on a snare drum

Stanza 3

describes the harbour beyond the reflection of the street lights and the 'ceaseless activity' of movement on the water as the ferry moves away

Stanza 4

describes the water activity, comparing it to chromosomes 'uniting and dividing', the part of the harbour where the yachts are moored with their masts sticking up like tomato stakes and the ferry moving on into the harbour

Stanza 5

describes the 'redness' of the city and the darkness between the bay that the ferry is leaving and the city beyond it

Stanza 6

describes the reflections of the long white lights which seem to be feeling over the surface of the water like a hand feeling in the darkness for a light switch

Stanza 7

describes the way that the ferry now 'wades' out into the harbour and is soon lost in the light from the Harbour Bridge

Stanza 8

likens this to a spectacular show (like those produced by Busby Berkeley, who produced lavish musical films during the period of the Great Depression in the 1930s) and the Harbour Bridge to a 'giant prop' in this show

Stanza 9

> explains that watching this ferry travel across the harbour makes the poet feel as if he is in a 'movie theatre', with the boat like some moth that is caught in the beam from the movie projector

Stanza 10

> comments that the poet will soon lose sight of the ferry, but his last view of it makes it look like 'honeycomb' filled with 'yellow light'

Analysis

The poet is exploring not only the scene with the ferry but also his perceptions of the ferry. The journey of the ferry is charted from the wharf out into the harbour and out of sight. The sense of the movement of the ferry on its course is structured in the quatrain stanzas. But there is a tension between the tight structure of the quatrain and the poet's use of enjambed lines that suggest the movement is thrusting beyond the parameters set down for it. For instance the lines:

> ... leaving this tuberous
> small bay, for the city

stretch across two stanzas, creating a sense of the ferry breaking out of the confines of the long narrow bay into the main harbour as it heads for the city. The ferry is described rather simply in terms of its movement — 'is leaving', 'goes up', 'wades' and is 'wandering'. But the images adumbrate as they are picked up in the images that surround the ferry.

The most significant of these images is that of the harbour itself. The harbour is initially described as 'huge' and 'dark'. The image of darkness is repeated in the description of the 'dark water', the 'empty dark', the 'blackness' and the final reference to 'darkness'. It is the darkness which provides a backdrop for the light and activity. The poet comments that he can see the ferry 'while it's on darkness'. The darkness becomes a kind of framing for the movement.

The contrasting images of light are very strong in this poem. The main image of light is concentrated on the ferry itself. This image likens the ferry to 'honeycomb' that is 'filled' with 'yellow light'. This is a warm image of multiple lights that seem almost to be oozing onto the water. But there are several other images of light that are juxtaposed with this image which come only at the end of the poem. One of these images is that of the 'street lights'. Their light is likened to a 'fluorescence' suggesting a luminosity and radiant emission of light across the water. This is amplified in the image of the 'neon redness'.

The light of the moored yachts is described as 'orange' and included in the metaphor of the yachts as a 'tomato stake patch'. Another image of light is that of the 'neon redness' and the 'longer white lights' that are out in the main part of the bay. Here the image of light intensifies so that it is described as a 'blizzard of light' that is 'swarming under the bridge'. Here the image of light is magnified as it includes the allusion to the 'Busby Berkeley spectacular'. This reference to the Depression musicals directed by Busby Berkeley, which offered spectacular film entertainment with abundant numbers of chorus girls who sang and danced their way through brightly lit escapist movies, introduces an element of unreality into the picture.

Set alongside these images of light is a sound image of the 'palm tree tops' which are likened to the 'touches of the brush on a snare drum in the windy night'. This soft abrasive sound seems to beat out the tempo for the movement of the ferry. The image of the activity on the water is likened to the movement of 'chromosomes uniting and dividing' and communicates a sense of rhythmic pulsating. This is further reinforced in the image of the light that 'trembles down into the water as if into ice'.

The place of the poet in the poem is also important. He describes his own role in watching the movement of the ferry. At the beginning of the poem he establishes that he 'stay[s] to watch' and at the end of the poem he returns with 'I'll lose sight' and 'I can see'. In one sense the poem is about what the poet sees from his vantage point on 'the balcony'. As he watches the play of light upon the water as the ferry moves towards the city the poet generalises his response — 'one does seem in a movie theatre'. The boat seems to be 'small as a moth/wandering through the projector's beam'. This sense of the unreality of the scene is brought back to reality with the final image as the poet notes: 'I'll lose sight of the ferry soon'.

This poem moves in an almost cinematic way as it traces the orbit of the ferry across the harbour. The vivid images flash before the reader's gaze just as the ferry has passed before the poet's view. Ultimately the poem revolves around the poet's own observations of himself observing the ferry.

Activity

Using the description and analysis in this study guide **and** your own reading of the poem make your own set of notes that answer these questions:

- **what** issues and ideas is the poem communicating?
- **what** feelings or emotions about these ideas are expressed?
- **how** are these expressed in the poetic form, features, techniques and devices?

Flames and Dangling Wire

This poem is written in irregular stanzas that resemble free verse. It paints a grim and challenging picture of the way in which we dispose of our waste products at the dump.

Description

The following outline of the subject of the poem shows you how the poet's ideas are structured. You should use it to help you in your first reading of the poem and then explore and analyse how the poet expresses these ideas and feelings.

Stanza 1

> establishes the setting of the poem, 'an always burning dump', situated 'on a highway' and 'over the marshland' with the fires of the dump burning in 'fingers' across the space

Stanza 2

> establishes this setting as not far from the city, which the poet describes as being 'like stakes in the earth'
>
> describes a waterbird that takes off from the swamp and likens its movement to that of a turtle on 'the Galapagos shore'

Stanza 3

> describes the way in which the air 'wobbles' and a 'fog' seems to cover the sun with the transmitted heat from the dump

Stanza 4

> describes the way the smoke seems to make the distant city buildings seem like stencils and the landscape is covered with tins and the wrecks of car bodies protruding from the sand dunes

Stanza 5

> describes the 'shadowy figures' moving in this landscape and suggests that they look as if they are trying to identify 'the dead'

Stanza 6

> expands the image of the dead and those engaged in 'forking over rubbish'
> describes the sour smoke that 'is hauled out' and the scavengers who are also moving in this landscape

Stanza 7

> begins an analogy with hell and the devils who would 'pick about through our souls' for something to feed from

Stanza 8

> continues the analogy, saying that the figures in this landscape seem to be wandering in the same kind of eternity searching for 'some peculiar sensation'

Stanza 9

> describes how the poet and his companion get out and move in this landscape (and as they do so they are hit by the smell that is 'huge') and the physical reality of the rotting rubbish

Stanza 10

> expresses the realisation that the poet is, in
> one sense, standing 'in the future' with the
> city appearing like a mirage and he is
> standing amongst 'things that worked'

Stanza 11

> describes a labourer who hoists stuff into the
> flames and a flapping that reminds the poet
> of the painting of *The Raft of the Medusa*

Stanza 12

> describes another man who seems like the
> man on the barge pole in the painting
>
> comments that it is a man who is 'wiping his
> eyes'
>
> comments that working here would make
> you weep

Stanza 13

> describes the poet's interaction with the man
> whose eyes are bloodshot and moist
>
> comments that this man could hardly avoid
> hatred, knowing what he does about
> humankind

Stanza 14

> describes an old radio from which wires are
> 'dangling'
>
> reflects that the voices that were once
> broadcast through this radio are still moving
> and speaking somewhere

Stanza 15

> continues the image of the voices that are still
> moving somewhere else in the universe, and
> the music and the sense of light that once was

Analysis

The poem begins with a truncated sentence that sets the scene for this poem 'over the marshland'. The image of the marshland suggests a wetland that is seen by humans as having no value and therefore to be the appropriate place for a dump. The opening of the poem contains a number of prepositional phrases that place the scene in its context before it is actually named: 'on a highway', 'over the marshland', 'off to one side' and 'in a row'. The statement 'it is an always-burning dump' following these phrases is a powerful image of the waste disposal. The personification of the smoke as 'fingers spread and dragged to smudge' and the 'gravel road' that approaches the dump emphasise the human intervention in this marshland. The smoke is also described, later in the poem, as 'sour' and likened to a 'rope' that is 'hauled out everywhere'.

The image of the dump is contrasted with images of the city as 'driven like stakes into the earth', suggesting a starkness and firmness that is used to elaborate on the landscape and atmosphere of the dump. The city 'buildings' are described as becoming 'stencilled in the smoke', suggesting that only their outlines are visible as the smoke rises and creates a 'mirage' of a city that no longer seems to exist.

The landscape of the dump is vividly portrayed 'rolling in its sand dune shapes'. In this 'landscape of tin cans' and 'cars like skulls' the poet sees a vision of hell that turns into a vision of the future. This hell, portrayed in the image 'vast grey plastic sheets of heat' is inhabited by 'shadowy figures' clad 'in overalls and goggles' whose task is to identify the dead. Their task is carried out at the 'dampened fires' where they are engaged in 'forking over rubbish'. As well as these shadowy figures whom the poet describe as 'devils', there are the 'scavengers' who also scour the rubbish in the dump. These scavengers are seen to be searching for 'vestiges of appetite with which to stimulate themselves'. The poet identifies this task as occurring in 'eternity'.

The labourers in the dump become the focus of the poet's attention. The description of each one acts as a vignette. One draws upon the allusion to the painting *The Raft of the Medusa*. This painting by the French Romantic painter Théodore Géricault (1791–1824) tells the story of the foundering of the *Medusa* as a result of a series of bunglings on the coast of Africa with the cost of many lives. The painting depicts the scene in oils on a large canvas in which the figures of the dead and dying are piled on a makeshift raft with a flimsy sail billowing in the wind, while one figure signals desperately to a passing ship. The painting explores the idea of man's struggle against nature. This allusion suggests the desperation of the task being undertaken by the labourer. Another labourer is depicted as the 'demon with the long barge pole' suggesting the end of the world.

The main image of the dump is that of the radio — the 'dangling wire'. This image takes on symbolic significance as the poet reflects on the use to which it was once put. The radio once carried 'voices', 'horse-laughs' and 'Chopin', and these sounds are 'still travelling'. Thus, despite the destruction of the radio and all it once 'received', these sounds and voices are not dead.

The poet uses this notion of the present and the future to comment implicitly on the shape of the future. The 'huge' smell that is capable of 'blasting the mouth dry' and the piles of discarded rubbish, the 'tons of rotten newspaper' and the 'great cuds of cloth' suggest the detritus of humanity. The poem suggests that the future will be filled with 'things that worked'.

The image of the man weeping is a strong one that the poet uses to suggest the horror of this place.

This poem challenges the reader to assess many aspects of contemporary city life. The main focus of this challenge is the notion of detritus and the ways in which we handle or dispose of it. There is a strong sense of a future marred by the mistakes of the present. The vibrant images flash before the reader's eyes and evoke the same kinds of tears as those of the workers at the dump.

 ctivity

Using the description and analysis in this study guide **and** your own reading of the poem make your own set of notes that answer these questions:

- **what** issues and ideas is the poem communicating?
- **what** feelings or emotions about these ideas are expressed?
- **how** are these expressed in the poetic form, features, techniques and devices?

North Coast Town

This poem is about an Australian town on the north coast. It is written in six stanzas, each of four lines of irregular length.

Description

The following outline of the subject of the poem shows you how the poet's ideas are structured. You should use it to help you in your first reading of the poem and then explore and analyse how the poet expresses these ideas and feelings.

Stanza 1

sets the scene on the north coast with the poet standing beside the road at a petrol station with a locked toilet and a hamburger stand that is also closed

comments that the poet has nothing in his pockets but 'sand'

Stanza 2

describes how he washes at a tap that is beside the 'changing sheds' and steps on mud and smells the stale smell of toilets and urinals

Stanza 3

describes how the poet eats an apple that is 'floury' and with the sand and palm fronds he indicates to each car that goes past his desire for a lift

Stanza 4

recounts how one car eventually slows and the poet runs towards it

describes the two men as 'hoods' who are 'going shooting'

describes their tattoos and the way that they rev the car and toss an empty can out onto the road

describes the country town

Stanza 5

describes features of the town — someone washing the pavement as they drive through; their reflection showing in the glass of the windows; the smoke from the exhaust trailing behind them

Stanza 6

> comments that this town is a 'warehouse
> picture show'
>
> recounts how they pass beyond the town
> itself into the 'bulldozed acres' where a new
> housing estate is being erected — 'making
> California'
>
> comments that they pass 'an Abo' who is
> 'not attempting to hitch' out of the town

Analysis

The poet sets the scene in this poem with the two truncated sentences. These establish the sense of the place and time and the poet's state of mind. There is a conversational sense to the poem, almost as if the poet is speaking in short bursts, rather than in any connected conversation.

This poem consists of snapshot-like images of the country town loosely linked with the narrative thread of the poet hitching a ride out of town. The key images of the town 'first thing in the morning' suggest desertion and include the 'Shell station', whose Men's toilets are 'locked', and the 'closed hamburger stand'. These images suggests a lack of trust within the town. Moreover they reinforce the criticism, which comes in the final comments, of the Americanisation of the town. This criticism is contained in the images of 'chrome', 'tile-facing', 'plate-glass' and 'they're making California'.

There is a diurnal time rhythm in the poem that begins with the early morning start and moves to a mid-morning peak. This rhythm is established through the actions of the poet. Each of these actions is contained in separate stanzas. The second stanza is concerned with the poet's morning ablutions. The image of washing 'at a tap beside the changing sheds' with its muddy puddle that he steps about on is juxtaposed with the image of the 'smell of the vandals' lavatory'. This image of vandalism suggests the reason that the Shell station locks its toilet doors overnight. The 'automatic chill' from the urinal is another contrasting image of the town. The next phase in the rhythm of the morning is concerned with standing at the roadside. Here the poet eats his 'floury apple' while he waits for a lift. The movement at this stage is slow and rhythmical and concerned with the movement of sand and 'palm fronds' and the 'warming-up' of the traffic as cars begin to pass. There is an accelerating movement here as a car approaches and stops. The image of the 'hoods' catapults the reader into a new speed zone, as the poet passes through the town.

The description of the 'hoods' is captured in short snapshots of the 'tattoos', their 'greasy Fifties pompadour', their noisy run down the main street and their drinking — 'drop their first can'. This image suggests two less than savoury characters who are 'going shooting'. Nevertheless, the poet paints a somewhat compassionate picture of the pair against the setting of the town.

The key images of the town suggest the same kind of degradation that the poet suggests in the 'hoods'. There is nothing subtle about this town. It has taken on board the more garish and superficial aspects of American commercialism. This is signalled in images such as 'plastic pennants', 'pink "Tropicana" motel', the 'RSL, like a fancy-dress Inca' and the 'Coronation', which is described as a 'warehouse picture show'.

The most significant image is that of the 'bulldozed acres'. This image of destruction from which further 'development' is to occur is stated simply and starkly. The juxtaposition of this statement with the image of the 'Abo' who is 'not attempting to hitch' in the final line gives it a powerful force. The understatement somehow highlights the horror of the situation.

Gray is presenting a vibrant set of images that ask the reader to re-examine what it happening to this north coast town. There a sense of sorrow for the loss of what once was, although this is not specified. Instead the reader is offered a critical account of what is. This account suggests a loss of trust and humanity as the town is taken over.

Using the description and analysis in this study guide **and** your own reading of the poem make your own set of notes that answer these questions:

- **what** issues and ideas is the poem communicating?
- **what** feelings or emotions about these ideas are expressed?
- **how** are these expressed in the poetic form, features, techniques and devices?

Journey: The North Coast

This poem describes the poet's experience of a train journey from the city to the north coast. The poem begins in the middle of the journey and describes the actions and feelings of the poet as he moves away from the city to the north coast town.

Description

The following outline of the subject of the poem shows you how the poet's ideas are structured. You should use it to help you in your first reading of the poem and then explore and analyse how the poet expresses these ideas and feelings.

lines 1–5	recount the poet waking in his bunk (which is swaying with the movement of the train as if it were an old sailing ship in the sea) and the noise of the train tearing along the tracks, which seems to be ripping the wind
lines 6–7	explain that the man who has occupied the lower bunk has gone
lines 7–10	describe how the poet swings himself out and pushes the window sash up so that sunlight comes in as he moves round on the carpet of the carriage
lines 10–12	describe the way that the water moves in the basin and how it seems to join together as he washes his hands in its coldness
lines 13–15	comment on the view that he can see from this position and how that reminds him of things from his past
lines 16–22	describe the movement of the train and the way its shadow passes on the parts of the landscape that they are passing, including the paddocks, fences, ferny creek banks and burnt tree trunks
lines 23–29	recount how the train moves on down the slope and then bursts into the light of the beach which seems to make the train compartment 'whirl' with the pattern of light and shade
lines 29–32	recount how the poet looks at himself in the mirror and decides to leave his hair 'ruffled', then puts away the other items that belong to him

| lines 32–36 | comment that now the poet can close the suitcase that has stood for the past year on top of the wardrobe in a 'furnished' room |

Analysis

This poem presents an account of the poet's journey by train to the north coast. The poem commences somewhere into the journey with the poet waking from sleep in the early morning. The main images of the poem include the images of the train and the countryside. These are juxtaposed with the actions of the poet.

The opening image of the train likens it to a 'clipper', the grand old sailing boats that once plied the seven seas. The metaphor of the train as a 'clipper' is extended from the swaying movement to the sounds that it makes and the train's interaction with the wind — 'it tears the wind apart'. There is a sense of power and majestic movement as the train rushes on its journey to the north coast. The train's shadow is then likened to a 'bird's' and this shadow 'flees on the blue and silver paddocks'. The lightness and swiftness of the train's movement are stressed in this image.

The inside of the train is not so majestic, with its 'drab carpet' and rattling sash. Although it does contain a 'silver basin', the water is icy cold. This idea is communicated in the metaphor — 'it joins together through my hand'. The interior is, however, filled with light that is at times 'sunlight rotating' and at other times is 'strewn with flakes of light that make the whole compartment whirl'. These light images suggest a sense of freedom as the poet travels north. This feeling of freedom is reinforced through the images of the countryside.

The first image of the countryside is captured in the metaphor 'bright crockery days', which suggests lightness and homeliness.

The colour of the paddocks, 'blue and silver', reinforces the feeling of calm and serenity in the landscape. The fences are described through the analogy 'look split from stone', giving them a solidity that is softened by the images of 'banks of fern' which suggest antiquity and softness. The richness of the landscape is suggested in the catalogue of images that establishes this richness. The colours of the bank — 'red' — and the creek — 'dark' — suggest a depth that is further reinforced by the image of the creek 'full of roots' and with 'logs and leaves suspended'. There is also a lusty sensuousness in the images of the 'slender white gum trees' that move down the slopes 'as a nude descends a staircase'.

The contrasting imagery of the seascape is contained in the grammatical metaphor, 'bursts open on the sea'. This image extends and returns to the clipper image of the opening of the poem. The movement of the sails of the clipper is echoed in the way the 'calico beach' is 'unfurling'. This explosion of light into the train marks the end of the journey for the poet.

The poet's emotional journey reflects the physical journey through the landscape. The poem begins somewhere towards the middle of this journey with the poet waking from sleep to discover the absence of the man who had occupied the bunk below him. The poet 'swing[s] out' of his own bunk to open the window onto the scene outside. The poet's actions are those simple common ones of washing, dressing and packing his belongings into the 'case' ready for the arrival. Using a homely image, the poet indicates his decision to leave his hair 'rufffled a bit that way'.

This overnight trip has brought the poet into the light of the north coast. As he looks out and sees what is ahead, he also reflects on the past 'twelve months'. Here he continues the image of watching and explains that he has 'watched' this suitcase 'above the wardrobe in a furnished room' with a sense of anticipation of this journey. The reference to the furnished room emphasises the sense of the journey taking the poet home, or at least back to some part of the world that he associates with home.

This poem leads the reader to an uplifting ending as the journey moves towards its destination. Although the poem begins in the middle of the physical train journey, there is a sense in which the poet's emotional journey actually began a year ago. The poet experiences a sense of freedom and delight as he moves closer to his destination.

ctivity

Using the description and analysis in this study guide **and** your own reading of the poem make your own set of notes that answer these questions:

- **what** issues and ideas is the poem communicating?
- **what** feelings or emotions about these ideas are expressed?
- **how** are these expressed in the poetic form, features, techniques and devices?

Writing about the poet

After studying each poem individually it is important that you consider the commonalities in the ideas, feelings and poetic features of the poems that you have studied by the one poet. You can do this by considering the following general questions about all the poems and writing notes in answer to the questions using a range of poems to justify your general statements.

- What subjects and ideas does the poet explore in the poetry?
- What emotions or feelings does the poet express in the poetry?
- What forms and structures does the poet commonly use?
- What techniques or devices does the poet commonly use to encapsultate these ideas and feelings?

You should then write an essay such as the following that deals with the poems of this poet in a general way:

- 'Gray's poetry is remarkable for the vibrancy of image and depth of feeling.' Is this your view of Gray's poetry?

In answering this question you need to:

- define what you mean by 'vibrancy of image'
- define what you mean by 'depth of feeling'
- determine what you mean by remarkable
- select two poems that allow you to evaluate the truth of the statement
- develop an argument that either supports, negates or qualifies the statement

Preparing for the Examination

Introduction

Once you have studied all the poems set for each poet, it is important that you consider the two poets you are studying *in relation to one another*. While the two poets may be different in various ways there will also be some areas of similarity. It is important that you identify these areas. You may not necessarily be required to compare and contrast the poets in an examination question. However, by noticing the similarities and differences, you will also become more aware of the individuality of each poem and poet within the great poetic traditions. Consequently, you will become more aware of the ways in which poetry, in general, works. This is important because many of the questions allow you to discuss this in relation to the two poets you have studied.

There are different ways in which you can examine the poets side by side. You could, for instance, compare and contrast individual poems by the two poets in terms of:

- subject
- ideas
- feelings
- voice of the poet
- structure and form
- patterns of imagery
- poetic devices
- language features

You may find it helpful to compare and contrast these features for different pairs of groups or poems by each of the poets. This exercise also helps you identify the poems that you know well and those to which you may need to give additional attention.

One of the most effective ways to record this information is to draw up a table with a column for each poem. The table on the following page illustrates the way in which you could draw up a summary of the poems. You should use this as a model for the particular poems that you are studying. Be sure to identify the main ideas in each poem, the mood and the poetic techniques that the poet has used to communicate his or her ideas. Remember to include quotes to support the information in your table.

Writing about the two poets

Ultimately, you will be required to write about the two poets in the one essay. This will commonly involve writing about one poem from each of the poets, although it is possible that you could be asked to write about more than one poem by each poet. It is important that you prepare yourself to write on all poems, as it is possible for the examiners to specify the poems that they wish you to write about. There are basically three ways in which you can write this kind of essay:

- two mini essays connected in the middle
- comparing and contrasting features of the two poems
- integrating information about both poems throughout your answer.

The particular essay structure you choose will depend upon the question that you are asked and the ease with which you are able

Chart summarising key features of four poems

Orb Spider	Kubla Khan	Out Out —	Late Ferry
meditation	'psychological curiosity' fragment	dramatic monologue	imagistic
poet as subject 'I saw her'	visitor from Porlock interrupts creation of poem dreamed	Macbeth allusion 'Out, out brief candle'	Poet's perception of scene described 'I sat to watch'
all in the natural world is sacred 'one perfect drawing'	the creative process 'a mighty fountain momently was forced'	insignificance of life 'Little-less-nothing'	the play of light and dark 'orange lights', 'empty dark'; sound and silence 'brush on a snare drum'
images of spider spinning web 'pegging out her web'; cosmological image of web 'a simple cosmography'; image of insects 'clicked like opening seed-pods'; image of flowers 'bright marigolds'; images of minute bodies orbiting the world 'planetismal beauty'	images of Kubla Khan Alph 'the sacred river'; countryside through which the river runs 'blossomed many an incense-bearing tree', 'twice five miles of fertile ground', woman wailing for her demon lover' and 'damsel with a dulcimer'	image of saw personified 'as if to prove saws knew'; image of hand 'holding up the hand'; image of sister 'in her apron'; image of doctor 'put him In the dark of ether'; image of the landscape 'five mountain ranges'	images of ferry and its movement 'trembles', 'swarming'; images of harbour 'huge dark harbour'; images of light 'longer white lights feel nervously'; image of sounds, e.g. palm tree tops
three parts: spider spinning web, significance for poet, significance for wider world 'immovable stars'	two parts: source of creativity 'caverns measureless to man', intuitive nature of creative process 'he on honey dew hath fed'	single stanza moves with mood of events 'So. But the hand was gone already.'	tightly structured quatrains using enjambed lines 'The ferry wades now into the broad/open harbour'
verbs associated with the poet's thinking 'I saw', 'I watched', 'she taught me'	sensuous sounds and rhythms 'five miles meandering with a mazy motion'	half rhyme 'load'/'said'; simple diction 'day was all but done'; colloquial language 'Call it a day'	rhythm of ferry's movement contrasted with images such as 'Busby Berkeley spectacular'

to make comparisons and contrasts or integrate information. While it may sometimes appear easier to write about each poem separately, it is very difficult to sustain a detailed argument in this style of writing, given the limited time and space available to you in the examination. However, it is important that you have practised all three styles of essay to enable you to make a choice in the examination that best suits your skills and knowledge, the particular poet studied and the question being asked.

Writing two mini essays

Writing two 'mini essays' means essentially writing one essay with two distinct sections, each one dealing with one of the two poems. The two mini essays would each contain your discussion of the salient aspects of the individual poems. Essentially this would contain discussion of 'what' the poem is saying and 'how' it says it. This might fall neatly into one extended paragraph on each aspect for each poem, or it might have two or more less extensive paragraphs on each aspect for each poem. The essay would contain an introduction and a conclusion. To help make a neat structure there may be a linking paragraph or sentence between the two 'mini essays'. The following plan shows how this might look in practice.

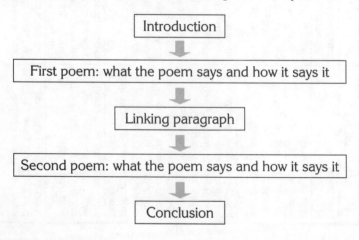

Introduction

First poem: what the poem says and how it says it

Linking paragraph

Second poem: what the poem says and how it says it

Conclusion

This essay structure would be appropriate for a question such as:

'Poetry expresses ideas and feelings in concentrated forms.' Discuss two poems that you have studied in the light of this statement.

In answering this question you would need to:

- decide what you mean by the terms 'ideas', 'feelings' and 'concentrated form'
- select the two poems (one from each poet) that demonstrate your notion of ideas and feelings
- determine how the poet has expressed these ideas and feelings in a concentrated form.

Your introduction would include your definition of ideas, feelings and concentrated form and would identify the poems that you intend to discuss. Your introduction might look something like this:

Poetry is sometimes concerned with ideas that are of a personal nature and, at other times, with ideas of a more public or social nature. In both cases poems express feelings about these ideas and feelings, often in a form that compresses and shapes language in various ways so that the imagery is more vividly conveyed. In Judith Beveridge's poem, 'The Domesticity of Giraffes', a public issue relating to the incarceration of wild animals in a zoological park is explored and we feel with the poet the sense of pathos for these animals as she exposes their situation in a verse form that is as tightly controlled as the giraffe's own enclosure. By contrast, Robert Gray's poem, 'Dyptich', expresses his personal view of his parents and his feelings about each of them as he looks back at childhood experiences of his parents from the adult perspective. His ideas and feelings are also expressed in a tightly controlled poem that resembles the two-leaved painting — dyptich — that is commonly found on an altar.

Your choice of poems will depend upon the nature of the question and the particular way in which you define the key concepts in the question. Some poems will better suit one type of definition while other poems will best suit other definitions. Thus, for instance, should you chose to define 'concentrated form' as stanza structures, a poem such as 'Late Ferry' would be a better choice than 'Dyptich'. Similarly if 'feelings' included the poet's feelings about his or her personal experiences, 'Fox in a Tree Stump' would be a better choice than 'The Domesticity of Giraffes'. Your personal definition of the key terms in the question is vital in allowing you to control the direction of your essay.

Once you have made this choice, you can shape your essay. For each poem you will discuss the ideas, the feelings expressed in the poem and the ways in which the concentrated form is used to express these ideas and feelings.

To link the two parts of the essay a sentence or paragraph may be necessary to avoid the abrupt switch from one poem to the next. This paragraph may begin with connecting words that indicate either similarities or differences in the ways in which the poems work. Words that indicate similarities include 'similarly', 'likewise', 'in the same way', and so on. Words that indicate difference include 'by contrast', 'on the contrary', 'on the other hand' and so on. The linking paragraph should show the connection between the ideas, feelings and forms of the two poems. It will, of necessity, be short but will make a smooth transition between the discussion of the two poems. It might look something like this:

> While Beveridge expresses her feelings of empathy for the animals in their enclosure in tightly structured stanzas, Gray allows us to wander over the two leaves of the diptych that contain the two portraits of his parents. He depicts his

feelings about his parents as he presents the anecdotes that help him to recreate their images.

The linking paragraph works as a kind of conclusion to the first mini essay and an introduction to the second mini essay.

A conclusion to the essay is required to complete the pattern. The conclusion will be relatively brief and will bring together the main ideas that have been explored in a 'big picture' way. It might, for instance, look like this:

> Both Gray and Beveridge explore issues and ideas of personal concern to them. For Beveridge the issues are related to the wide world of animals and humans, while for Gray the concern is with his personal interactions with his parents. Both poets rely on images to express these ideas and their feelings about them, and on the manipulation of poetic forms. By concentrating the form they are able to highlight their ideas and feelings.

Comparing and contrasting features of the two poems

You might be specifically required to write this type of essay; alternatively, it would be an appropriate way in which to organise your discussion of the two poems according to the question. An essay that asks you to compare and contrast features of the poem might be organised in a number of ways. This will, in part, depend on the question, the particular poems and the aspects on which you are going to focus. It could use the same format that we have just seen in the two mini essays, or it may use other structures. In any case the key element that you will be concerned with is what each poem is saying and how it says it. A possible structure might be:

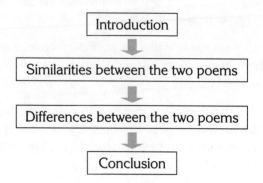

This type of structure might be appropriate for a question such as:

> 'Poetry is concerned with image not action.'
> Do you agree? Discuss this statement in relation to two poems that you have studied by different poets.

In answering this question you would need to:

- decide what you mean by the terms 'image' and 'action'
- select two poems that have these elements as you define them
- decide how image works in the two poems
- decide how action works in the two poems
- compare and contrast the two poems in the light of these concepts.

Your introduction would include your definition of image and action and outline the key features of image and action in the two poems. You might, for instance, decide that image is concerned with the visual pictures that the poet creates through a variety of poetical devices and that action is concerned with the actions that characters carry out in the poem, or things which happen to them. You will introduce these ideas and relate them to the two poems which you intend to discuss. Your introduction might look like this:

> Poetic images encapsulate the key ideas that a poet wishes to communicate in a metaphorical way within the form of a poem. However, they are not the only way in which ideas are communicated in poetry. While concerned with the poet's experience, poems may also feature characters who engage in specific actions or who are the objects of the actions of others. Poets use both these devices to communicate their ideas and feelings with different results. Coleridge presents the reader with a plethora of images in his conversational poem, 'This Lime-tree Bower my Prison', to communicate his ideas about the life of the Imagination and Nature as the Great Universal Teacher. Nevertheless, his poem is not without actions that are carried out by the characters involved. Frost, on the other hand, relies upon the action of the saw and the various actions of the characters in his poem, 'Out out —', to communicate his idea about the transience of life, but his poem is not without vibrant images.

The first part of the essay will deal with the use of images in the two poems and the ways in which they contribute to the main ideas and the poet's feelings about these ideas. This may be structured so that the images are dealt with in separate paragraphs or the similarities in the use of imagery may be dealt with within the same paragraph.

The next section of the essay will deal with the ways in which the poets use action in their poems. As these poets use action in different ways, your essay will present the differences rather than the similarities between them. You may structure this so that the actions are dealt with in separate paragraphs, or you may include discussion of the contrasting uses of action within the same paragraph.

The actual elements you deal with will depend on the particular poems that you have chosen and the ways in which you approach discussion of each. The conclusion will bring the main ideas of your argument together and will demonstrate how the similarities and differences contribute to the poem's effectiveness. A conclusion might look something like this:

> Both these poets make use of image and action to communicate their ideas and feelings. For Coleridge the images express key elements of his view of the natural world whereas, for Frost, the images of the machinery (which is given human qualities) help to communicate his ideas about the transience of life as the youth is cut down before his prime. Both poets also use action to communicate their ideas. For Coleridge the action is more a mental action that allows him to recreate in his imagination the situation of his friend's ramble through the countryside. In Frost's poem, on the other hand, there is physical action as the boy's hand is cut and his life expires as other characters attempt to revive him. Both poets, nevertheless, use both image and action to express their ideas.

An integrated essay

You might be specifically required to write this type of essay or it may be an appropriate way in which to organise your discussion of the two poems according to the question. This type of structure allows you to write about both poems as you develop an argument in response to the main ideas identified in the question. Both poems are used to illustrate the stages in your argument. The argument is likely to be developed in relation to some general notions relating to the ideas and techniques of poetry. It might be an appropriate response to a question such as:

> 'The most effective poems vividly convey ideas and feelings.' How do they do this?

In answering this question you will need to:

- decide what you mean by 'ideas' and 'feelings'
- decide what you mean by 'vividly convey'
- determine which poetic features best illustrate how poems vividly convey ideas and feelings
- decide which poems you will use to illustrate your argument.

The introduction will outline what you mean by 'ideas' and 'feelings' and identify what these are in the specific poems that you have selected. It will also explain what you mean by 'vividly convey' and identify the techniques that you intend to discuss in your essay. It might look something like this:

> Poetry is concerned with ideas of a personal nature that show the poet's privately held views about a particular idea or issue. A distinguishing feature of poetry is its capacity to communicate the feelings and emotions that a poet has about these ideas or issues. These aspects are communicated to the reader or listener through the structure of the poem (in which ideas are compressed in images to highlight their intensity) and through the sound qualities of the words in the rhythmic patterns within the lines of verse. The poets, Beveridge and Coleridge, both communicate their ideas about their place in the universe in poems that are very different in form; furthermore, they are separated by a continent and more than a century in time. Nevertheless both poets draw upon the images and the play of sound to communicate their ideas and feelings in 'Orb Spider' and 'The Aeolian Harp'.

The main part of the essay will pick up on the aspects that are highlighted in this introduction. One paragraph, for instance, might delineate what you mean by the ideas about the poet's place in the universe. This will include discussion about both poems within the paragraph. Another paragraph would include discussion about the feelings that are expressed by the poets towards their ideas, and would include discussion of both poems in the one paragraph. Another would include discussion of the images used by both poets and the ways that these compress the ideas in the poems. A further paragraph would include discussion of the sound qualities of the poems and the ways in which these help to communicate the ideas and feelings. You would also devote a paragraph to the rhythmic patterns and the lines of verse and stanza structures and the ways in which these help to communicate the meaning. Your concluding paragraph would include some judgement about the effectiveness of these poems in vividly conveying the poet's feelings and ideas.

Conclusion

Whatever essay structure you use will ultimately depend upon the examination question and your skills in using your knowledge about the poems to construct a reasonable argument in answer to the question. It is important that you have developed your own interpretation of the poems that you are studying and that you are able to articulate these interpretations within the scope of the question.

Remember there is a wide range of 'right' answers and very few answers that can be argued to be wrong — as long as you are mindful of the structure and grammar of the poem. While it is possible, for instance, to focus on a particular issue within any poem and to base a discussion around it, it is important that you ensure that your ideas are able to be supported with evidence from the poem itself, and do not include extraneous impressions that cannot be supported by evidence from the text.

Similarly, when examining the two poets side by side, while there are many similarities and differences between them, it is important that you focus on the significant ones, rather than attempting to make superficial comparisons. For instance, to identify Coleridge's poems as containing images of nature and Gray's poems as also containing images of nature is not to say very much at all. If you notice that both poets use such images, you need to examine what these images represent in terms of each poet's ideas and feelings and how they are constructed within the form of the poem and the meanings that emanate from this.

This type of study can be very rewarding, particularly as it gives you greater insight into the ways in which poetry works. Ultimately, you are left with the task of answering those very basic questions:

> what is the poem saying?
> how does it say it?

Remember that, although you read the poem on the page, poetry is in the final analysis a sensuous experience of thought and feeling and you need to be aware of the flow and feel of the poem in order to fully understand its mood and meaning.

Practice essays

Make plans for, and write, the following essays referring to at least two poems by different poets in each essay. You may wish to try out different essay structures for each essay to be sure that you can adapt your interpretation and knowledge of the poems to various types of questions.

1. **'The task of the poet is to allow the reader to see familiar situations in unfamiliar ways.' Discuss the ways in which the two poets achieve this goal in one poem by each poet.**

In this essay you should include discussion of:

- what you mean by 'familiar situations'
- what you mean by 'unfamiliar ways'

- the familiar situation in each poem
- the unfamiliar way in which the poet presents it
- the ways in which the poet allows the reader to see this.

2. **'The most effective poems leave the sound and the image lingering in the reader's memory.' Show how two of the poems that you have studied by two different poets achieve this affect.**

In this essay you should include discussion of:

- what you mean by 'the sound' in a poem
- what you mean by 'the image' in a poem
- the particular sounds and sound patterns in each of the two poems
- the particular images in each of the two poems
- how or why these remain in the memory.

3. **'Ultimately, poetry must present a personal account of human experience.' Discuss how two poems you have studied from two different poets achieve this.**

In this essay you should include discussion of:

- what you mean by 'personal account'
- what you mean by 'human experience'
- the particular human experience in each of the two poems
- the particular personal account offered by the two poets
- the techniques that each of the two poets has used to achieve this.

4. **'Poetry expresses the most private thoughts in a public form.' Discuss the ways in which two of the poems that you have studied achieve this.**

In this essay you should include discussion of:

- what you mean by 'most private thoughts'
- what you mean by 'public form'
- the thoughts in each of the two poems that you have selected
- the nature of the public form chosen by the poet
- the particular devices used by the poet in each of the poems.

5. **'It is impossible to appreciate a poem without exploring the techniques the poet has used to express ideas and feelings.' Discuss the ways that ideas and feelings are expressed by the poet in two of the poems you have studied.**

In this essay you should include discussion of:

- what you mean by 'ideas' in a poem
- what you mean by 'feelings' in a poem
- what techniques a poet uses to express these
- the specific ideas and feelings in the two poems that you have selected
- the particular techniques used by the poets in each of the poems to express these ideas and feelings.

Glossary

adumbrates   foreshadows or prefigures.

alliteration   the repetition of the same consonant sound in words in close proximity.

e.g.   'Between the sob and the clubbing of the gunfire'

assonance   the repetition of the same vowel sound in words in close proximity.

e.g.   'morning rolls them in the foam'

blank verse   unrhymed iambic pentameter. This is the main poetic form in which Shakespeare wrote most of his plays and his sonnets. The iambic foot consists of an unstressed followed by a stressed syllable. Blank verse contains five such feet.

coda   a more or less independent section of a piece of literature or music introduced to bring the piece to a close.

dramatic monologue   a poem that is a monologue spoken by a character in a particular situation. When a poet uses the dramatic monologue form he or she establishes a character who is speaking in the poem, and it is obvious that this character is not simply the personal voice of the poet. The monologue generally reveals a great deal about the character.

dulcimer   a zither with metal strings that is struck by a hammer.

enjambed   refers to lines of poetry where there is no punctuation marker at the end of the line. The sense therefore runs onto the next line. A tension is set up between the grammatical structures and the poetic structures. In reading the line it is important to keep the poetic rhythm while at the same time maintaining the flow of the meaning.

e.g.   I saw her, pegging out her web
thin as a pressed flower in the bleaching light.

fricative sounds   sounds made by the breath or voice scraping across the organs of articulation, i.e., the tongue, teeth, lips, soft palate and hard palate.

juxtaposed refers to the placing of two ideas or images together. Commonly, ideas or images are juxtaposed to show either their similarities or their differences.

e.g. 'She hung in the shadows as the sun burnt low ...'

monologue a long speech by a single character. This may be in poetry or in verse.

oxymoron a particular type of juxtaposition in which the two things juxtaposed are opposite. In an oxymoron the opposed things are commonly in the form of a noun and adjective, e.g. sweet sorrow, bitter sweet, exhilarating despair.

pantheism the doctrine that God does not exist as a personality but rather as the transcendent reality of the material world; i.e., that God exists everywhere in nature.

pastoral poems poetry that portrays rural life, usually in an idealised manner.

plosive sounds those sounds made by an explosion of breath or voice, e.g. p, b, t, d, h, k.

preceptor an instructor or teacher.

prepositional phrases a group of words introduced by a preposition, e.g. 'in a calm sea'.

quatrain refers to a stanza of poetry that contains four lines. The lines may be of a regular length and there are various ways in which each rhyme is used within the stanza.

rumination literally, chewing the cud; metaphorically, pondering over something.

sequacious following with smooth regularity.

subjective experience experience that is very personal.

truncated sentence a sentence which does not contain a finite verb, i.e. a verb that has a subject.

e.g. 'And this cobweb odour/of wet dust'

utopian refers to the notion of something that is perfect.

vignette a small, graceful literary sketch.